The
SHIPPING
BROKER

DEREK BERG

About the Author

The author was born in Hong Kong. His father was Norwegian; his mother, who died when he was three, was Australian.

Derek received his early education in China and was sent to Australia just before Japan's entry into World War II. There he completed his schooling.

He studied medicine at the University of Sydney. Following graduation he became a surgeon and later a radiotherapist.

The author, having written and self-published an autobiography has now written about life between the two great wars of the twentieth century as seen through the eyes of his father.

This book is the story of a segment of Sverre Berg's life, based on notes he wrote while a prisoner of war and later handed down to the author, his son.

Derek and his wife Judy moved to Noosa in south-east Queensland where they are enjoying their retirement.

Published in Australia by Sid Harta Publishers Pty Ltd,
ACN: 007 030 051
23 Stirling Crescent, Glen Waverley, Victoria 3150 Australia
Telephone: 61 9560 9920, Facsimile: 61 9545 1742
E-mail: author@sidharta.com.au

Telephone: 61 9560 9920, Facsimile: 61 9545 1742
E-mail: author@sidharta.com.au

First published in Australia 2008
This edition published August 2008
Copyright © Derek Berg 2008
Cover design, typesetting: Chameleon Print Design

Berg, Derek
The Shipping Broker
EAN13: 978-1-921362-07-1
ISBN: 1-921362-07-3
pp264

Dedication

I am grateful for all the help from my wife for typing the manuscript, from Danny Keating for help with my illustrations and from Valina Rainer for all the corrections. Finally I thank my publisher Sid Harta for their encouragement and the format of this book.

Contents

INTRODUCTION

Father tell a story that sons will still repeat
so long as in the Northland a youthful heart shall beat.

This book is based on my father's notes which he put together while a prisoner of war in Hong Kong (1941–1945). It is not the story of his life but covers the period between 1913 and 1941.

My father was Norwegian. He was born in 1892 and grew up in Trondheim, Norway. He spoke excellent English and had a wide vocabulary; nevertheless, his native tongue was Norwegian and this is reflected in some of his notes. Sections of this book are taken directly from these notes and I have presented them in their original form, as they were when he handed them down to me.

I have researched and included some of the momentous events that touched his life and were of great interest to him.

Sverre Berg was a self-made man, who in spite of a number of tragedies made a success of his life. He had two happy marriages. He, like so many of his countrymen, had a great love of the sea and the ships that sailed upon it. He served two kings (those of Norway and Great Britain) loyally and with distinction.

I have tried to select the most commonly used spelling for some Chinese, Russian and even Norwegian names. The island of Koh Phra, referred to in chapter 24, is now known as Koh Phra Thong or Golden Buddha Island, and is a popular tourist destination.

The times I have written about are very different from today. There were no televisions, microwaves, computers or antibiotics. The ships my father loved navigated the oceans with the aid of a sextant, a chronometer, a log towed from astern and admiralty charts. There was no such thing as 'SAT navigation'.

I have included a little of Norwegian history and legend, for this book is written in the hope that some of his grandchildren will enjoy reading of their grandfather, who was proud of his Norwegian heritage and lived in what to them would be a 'by-gone age'.
Derek Berg
Noosa 2007.

PART ONE

THE NORSEMAN, 1000AD

CHAPTER 1

THE VIKINGS

'From the Fury of the Northmen, deliver us, O Lord.'
– A monk's prayer

Twelve thousand years ago in the earliest post-glacial period, humans began wandering over Scandinavia, hunting, fowling and fishing. They later settled in the habitable areas, built skin boats and became adapt with bows, arrows, knives and harpoons. They domesticated the wolf (the first known domesticated animal) and buried their dead with their worldly goods in shallow graves.

We know little of their hardships but they did clear forests, plant crops and build crude stone and timber houses to shelter in. By 1500BC, village settlements became established and different dialects began to coalesce into one general language, Old Norse. Their writing was runic, they traded furs, timber, 'sea ivory' (walrus tusks and whale bone) and amber from the Baltic shore, with the peoples of southern Europe. Norsemen were sea and land traders long before they became Vikings (sea warriors).

Global Warming

From 800AD to 1300AD Europe experienced a climatic change with rising temperatures, referred to as the 'Medieval Warm Period'. This may well have been a global phenomenon. During this period Europeans began to enjoy unprecedented agricultural prosperity and as a result the population increased as the food supply became abundant. Great trading cities evolved (e.g. Venice, Amsterdam and London) and advances in technology led to the building of great cathedrals in western Europe.

It was during this warm period and the pressures associated with the increase in population that the Norsemen were stimulated to venture overseas and able to establish colonies in Iceland,

Greenland and even Labrador. It was a remarkable era of human progress, which occurred long before the Renaissance, and due in no small part to a very favourable climatic change.

To the ancients, the Etruscans, Greeks and Romans, Norway was a mythical land inhabited by giants and barbaric creatures, but saga, as well as the excavation of burial sites, indicates that these Norsemen were much more than primitive northern traders and warriors. These people had an eye for beauty: a beautiful sword; a beautiful ship; a beautiful horse; and, most of all, a beautiful woman. Combined with this ideal was an ideal of strength and courage. The sword must be keen, the horse strong and swift, the ship staunch and seaworthy and the women good and resilient.

Far from being unshaven and unwashed seamen, the Vikings used soap long before it was reintroduced into Europe after the fall of the Byzantine Empire. They commonly used combs, tweezers, razors and even 'ear spoons'. In England they had a reputation for cleanliness, insisting on bathing at least once a week – a practice almost unheard of in Anglo-Saxon England!

Most of all, these Norsemen had a great feel for the sea; in this they were supreme in Europe. They could sense the currents, winds, drifts and tides. They navigated by the stars at night and the sun by day. They had no knowledge of the magnetic compass yet they discovered the Shetlands, Hebrides, Faroes, Iceland, Greenland and Labrador. Indeed, the soul of the Viking lay within the sea and the Viking's longship.

These Norsemen were pagans and remained so, long after other Europeans had turned to Christianity. They grew up in a beautiful but harsh land and at an early age were exposed to the wild elements of nature and the furious passions of their fellow men to survive. Life was harsh and Norse beliefs reflected this harshness.

To the Norsemen, Odin ruled the heavens from Ascard with its great hall of Valhalla. Odin was the God of War and Knowledge. It was he who gave man the magical runic writing. Thor, his son, was the guardian of Ascard. He fought fierce giants and monsters. Thunder was the sound of his chariot as it crossed the heavens.

Odin's love of heroes led to the creation of the Valkyries, beautiful maidens who wore helmets and armour, carried spears and rode swift horses. The Valkyries were sent by Odin to ride over battlefields to carry away those slain warriors (Einherjars) whom Odin had chosen as worthy to join him in Valhalla, where they spent their days jousting and their nights feasting with fair maidens and listening to minstrels sing of past heroic deeds.

On earth, the dramatic landscape of Scandinavia, with its mountains of ice and snow, its deep blue fjords and seething springs shrouded in mist, were, to the Norsemen, populated by fearsome frost, storm and fire giants who roamed the forest and ice slopes while gentler mist maidens and elves dwelt near streams and lakes. In the underground caverns dwelt dark dwarfs and trolls. They were hideous creatures derived from the flesh of dead giants and because of their hideousness were condemned to live underground where they worked rich gems and beautiful ornaments. Any exposure to sunlight turned them instantly to stone.

Certainly this was the stuff of legends but, in truth, a dark and brutal set of beliefs. The gods were cruel taskmasters, demanding human sacrifices, accepting only the young and strong as suitable offerings.

In spite of these cruel beliefs, the victory of Christianity over paganism took much longer in Scandinavia than the rest of Europe and was not easily won. In the end it cost the lives of Norway's two greatest kings, Olaf Tryggvason and Saint Olaf Haraldsson, Norway's eternal king.

With the fall of the western Roman Empire (400AD), the Christian church remained the sole repository for learning, writing and worship in western Europe. But during the eighth century, western Europe and Christianity were threatened by the Moorish invasion from Africa, which was eventually checked by Charles Martel, King of the Franks in 732. Relief, however, was short lived. Sixty years later, Christian Europe was to receive another shock, this time from the pagan north.

On a misty July morning, strange longships appeared off Lindisfarne, a small island off the Northumberland coast of England. Bearded men with swords stormed ashore, plundered the rich monastery, slaughtered the cattle, killed many of the monks, then sailed away with a rich booty of gold, jewels, sacred emblems and the surviving monks for the

European slave markets. These were the first Vikings to plunder Europe and they were from Denmark.

The news of this atrocity spread throughout Christian Europe. It was to be the forerunner of many such raids, a taste of what was to come.

In 835 the Viking storm broke in its full fury on Europe. Fleets of longships, sometimes a hundred or more were rowed up the rivers of England, France and Russia or appeared off the coastal towns of Ireland and Scotland. Whole towns were occupied, their citizens slaughtered, women raped and treasures carried away.

Then, mercifully, another change occurred. Many of these Viking raiders decided to settle in the areas where they had once plundered; after all, the climate was less severe and the soil richer than that of their homeland. The Danes settled in England, the Norwegians in Scotland, the Faroes, Iceland and Greenland. The Viking Rollo acquired a slice of France – it was called Normandy; and eastward, Swedish Vikings settled in Russia and the Ukraine (Novgorod and Kiev).

These pagan Vikings succeeded in distracting and weakening life in Europe for 250 years (ten generations) before they settled down, established kingdoms and embraced Christianity. It was during the eleventh century that Viking activity began to wane. The death of Olaf in 1030, the death of Canute in 1032 and the climatic year of 1066 when the Norwegian Viking Harold Hardraade died at Stamford Bridge and William of Normandy defeated England's last Anglo-Saxon king, Harold II at Hastings – these all seemed to be defining events. There is little evidence of Viking activity after 1070.

The Norsemen

CHAPTER 2

SAINT OLAF

Olaf, Prince of Frey, was born a pagan in 995AD. Shortly after Olaf's birth, his father fell in love with the widowed Swedish queen who did not reciprocate his love. Nevertheless, he travelled to Sweden to seek her hand. She had him murdered, and Olaf was left to be brought up by his mother Aasta and a kindly stepfather.

Like many of his contemporaries, Olaf at a young age became a Viking – he sailed to England and assisted Ethelred (named the Unready) to oust the Danish Vikings from London and in doing so pulled down London Bridge (hence the nursery rhyme).

After two years in England, Olaf sailed to Normandy where he became impressed with Christianity and Ruda Cathedral (Rouen). He was baptised there in 1013 and vowed to one day build churches and Christianise Norway. But first, he wished to visit Jerusalem.

While sailing off Gibraltar, Olaf saw a vision that told him to return to Norway and establish a Christian kingdom, free of Danish and Swedish influences.

Olaf immediately turned north; he initially landed on the western shore of the Oslo fjord and later sailed to Nidaros (Trondheim) where he was accepted as king in 1015. He immediately set about rebuilding Nidaros, laid the foundation stone of a new church and set about replacing the old pagan beliefs with the Christian faith (the White Christ). Olaf had a reputation for being incorruptible and having a great belief in law and justice.

Olaf's first wife, Astrid, was the daughter of the Swedish king. She brought with her to Trondheim her handmaiden, a mystic, a fair and beautiful pagan, Alfhild. Astrid was unable to bear Olaf a child and Olaf, who was attracted to Alfhild, married her. (It was an old pagan custom and not uncommon for Vikings to have more than one wife.) Alfhild dutifully bore him a son. They called him Magnus and he eventually succeeded Olaf as King of Norway.

Like his great predecessor (Olaf Tryggvason), Olaf was opposed by the Danes, Swedes and those Norwegians who were in the pay of the Danish king (Canute, who was, in fact, a Christian) and by the many pagans in Norway who did not take kindly to Christianity.

In 1028 Canute, King of England and Denmark, moved north with a large fleet of Danish Vikings to reclaim his Norwegian colony. Olaf, with insufficient men and resources, was forced to flee with his little son Magnus across Sweden to the safety of relatives in northern Russia.

While in exile, Olaf had a dream telling him to return to Norway and reclaim his kingdom; so, leaving his son with relatives, he set off with a small band of followers across northern Russia, crossed the Baltic to Sweden and then marched through the forests to his old capital, Trondheim. As he travelled he recruited a small army of followers, but strenuously rejected all who retained pagan beliefs.

The nobles of the west, again supported by the Danes, were forewarned and assembled a large army based on Trondheim. On the morning of the 29 July 1030, the armies met at Stiklastad. It was an uneven contest and by day's end Olaf, aged thirty-five, was dead. Fighting to the last, wounded and pinned against a rock, with dead and dying comrades around him, he was struck by a spear hauled by a pagan, which, according to legend, carried a pagan curse.

Olaf's death meant that Norway reverted back to the rule of the Danish king, but after the battle, good men began to reflect and talked more and more of Olaf. They talked of his bravery and how bribery, disloyalty and paganism had combined to bring him down. They spoke of miracles, how the blood he shed while sliding down that rock with the cursed spear in his chest spilled onto his wounded followers and immediately restored them to health. They spoke also of how surviving victors and the vanquished carried his body to Nidaros for burial beside the river Nid, near the church he had built years before, and they remembered the words the Minstral Sigvert sang when he took up his harp over his friend's coffin.

This chest enshrines a heart of noble name
of one who freed his land from pagan bars.
May long the world his golden deeds proclaim,
his fame for ever written in the stars.

Eleven months later, Olaf's grave was opened, so that his remains could be transferred to a nearby church. To people's astonishment, the diggers found his body was perfectly preserved, his cheeks still rosy. Bishop Grimkell who was present declared Olaf a true saint and he was formally canonised by Pope Alexander III in 1164. Years later, his remains were moved yet again, this time to a crypt below the high altar of Nidaros Cathedral, the finest in all Scandinavia. To this very day it is said that even the sunlight glows more softly when touching the spot where Olaf lies.

It is of course true that, with time, legends grow and the number of miracles increase; but it is right and proper for all Norwegians to believe in them, for although King Olaf died against that rock at Stiklastad, Saint Olaf continues to live and work, giving hope to all that need it, well beyond the Viking age. He remains Norway's eternal king and saint. After some years, Magnus did become king of an independent Norway; he was followed by a number of Norwegian kings, all Christians, including Sverre (1184–1202) and Haaken (1217–1263), after which Norway and Sweden were united under Magnus VII. During the fourteenth century, the 'Black Death' decimated the population of Norway and later, in 1397, the whole of Scandinavia came under Danish rule (the Union of Kalmar or Calmar).

In 1523, Sweden gained her independence from Denmark and later cast covetous eyes on Norway. This lead to the Great Northern War (1703–1721), involving Denmark, Sweden and Russia. Denmark prevailed with Norwegian support; Sweden's ambitions for Norway were, for the time being, thwarted. This situation changed as a result of Denmark's support for France during the Napoleonic wars. Following the defeat of Napoleon at Waterloo, Norway was allocated to Sweden (Treaty of Keil). Later, as in Olaf's time, the Norwegians rebelled and gained some degree of autonomy, including their own parliament, 'The Storting'.

Finally, in 1905, a plebiscite was held and Norway at last gained full independence. Quite remarkably, given that Denmark was Norway's ancient enemy, Norway offered the crown to a Dane, Prince Carl of Denmark. He accepted and became King Haakon VII of Norway.

Reference: Maurice P. Dunlop, *Viking Knights: A Tale of the Pagan North* (Edinburgh, The Moray Press, 1933).

Trondheim (Nidaros) Cathedral

PART TWO

SCOTLAND, 1914

CHAPTER 3

GLASGOW

Sverre Berg, 1913

It is early February 1913 and the usual north Norwegian winter weather, the north westerly, is coming in through the fjord, blowing the snowflakes ahead of it. I am feeling none too grand in my pea jacket as I try to be brave and say a last farewell to my parents on that windy Brattor Wharf. They have just come ashore from the SS Haakon Jarl, the ship that is to take me to Newcastle (England) on my first trip abroad. I know what they are feeling; I can see Mother's troubled eyes and Father's questing look. He seems to know everyone in Trondheim and has just come out of the captain's cabin, no doubt getting his assurance that the weather is moderating, the ship won't sink and that we shall reach our destination in good time.

The hooter lets off a hiccup against the snowstorm, the deck hands take in the lines and we are off. I can see Father and Mother walking along the wharf keeping step with the ship, and we wave to each other until they come to the end of the wharf.

I go to my cabin. It is not luxurious, two bunks and not too much space, but to me at that time it was the threshold to wide horizons, the world and its wonders were going to be opened to me.

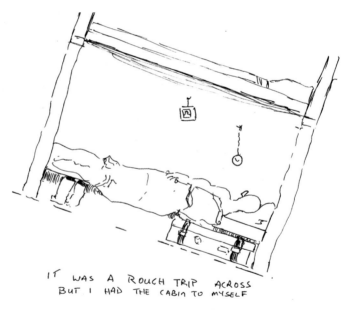

IT WAS A ROUGH TRIP ACROSS
BUT I HAD THE CABIN TO MYSELF

The author's impression

I have the cabin all to myself. As can be expected few people go travelling across the North Sea at this time of the year, and the passenger list is naturally skimpy, which is just as well. By the time my big trunk was manipulated into a corner there wasn't much room left. That trunk is really too cumbersome, too heavy and much too big to travel with, but it contains a lot of books; the Bergs have always been daft on books. I tidy up a bit, try to settle down, but find it difficult; the ship is not behaving well, and the air in the cabin is not good; it has that second hand feel about it, used last night and probably the night before that. The cabin is right aft, on top of the propeller and the steering engine. I am of course travelling steerage in what is essentially a coal fired cargo ship.

I decided to explore on deck and discovered a saloon, which is a good deal more pleasant. A couple of men were discussing the weather and fortifying themselves against it with aquavit and kindly offered me a dram, which I declined as I began to feel a bit drowsy and was sure a dram would not be very healthy. The three of us presently fell into an uneasy sleep in the saloon.

I do not know what the skipper told my father, but the weather did not moderate; on the contrary, it worsened a good deal by the time we left the fjord and got the full blast of the north westerly. However, I stayed on my legs, much to my surprise and to the surprise of some of the passengers, most of whom were unable to face dinner the first night out. The Norwegian coast is sheltered to a considerable extent by outlying islands and skerries, but there are gaps which allowed in the full force of the gale; it was then that the *Haakon Jarl* stood on her head.

The dining saloon was just below my cabin aft. Not very bright, it depended on oil lamps for illumination, electricity had not yet become standard equipment on many ships. Balanced lights were screwed into the bulkheads or tables, and with the rolling and bouncing about there was a constant flickering and dimming of the lights, which threw the saloon into an intermittent gloom.

It was a wet trip, but we eventually got to Bergen where we picked up some cargo and another passenger. However, I was still in occupation of my cubby-hole, when we left for the crossing to Newcastle.

The North Sea was true to form and we just staggered in. That was a ship I did not fall in love with.

From Newcastle I travelled by train to Edinburgh and then to Leith, in reality the port of Edinburgh on the southern shore of the Firth of Forth, where I had letters of introduction to Mr Peters, a prominent businessman and a friend of my previous employer. He had promised to look after me and see me started.

I was wise enough to leave my heavy luggage at Edinburgh Central Station and got a local train to Leith. Once at Leith and unsure of my whereabouts I had from time to time to ask my way.

While trudging along, humping my handbag, I came across a short bridge and then just ahead of me I saw a man with a drawn knife chasing a shrieking woman. He wasn't far behind her and I was expecting any moment to be an eyewitness to a grisly murder, for that was obviously what was going to happen. However, the tragedy resolved itself when two burly dock policemen spotted the couple, took up position and when they came near, plucked up the girl first, then the man, who of course was very drunk. It was rather a chastening experience for a newcomer in a strange land, and the sordid incident has stayed with me for many years.

Leith was not a success and Mr Peters suggested I go to Glasgow where there would be a better chance of finding the kind of work I was looking for. I was fortunate to obtain a position with a shipping firm in Glasgow covering insurance, forwarding, warehousing, shipping agencies and catering. It was a medium sized firm but an ideal training ground and its staff, first class. Mr Peters seemed to have a lot of interests in Glasgow, and it is no doubt due to his influence that I got this opening.

I received one pound a week as pay, which was perhaps generous, as I had discovered that my English was not as fluent as I thought it might be; perhaps the broad Scottish language has something to do with that? I payed eighteen shillings for board and lodging, so my budget was very finely balanced. I have my savings and my two scholarships, but I am afraid I shall have to gradually eat into these; but I am an optimist. I am at present full of youthful confidence. Incidentally, I get a shilling for overtime on Fridays to clear the mail, and I have found a young man to whom I am teaching the violin once a week – that brings in another bob; and hoping for more.

RMS Aquatania, 45,674 tons, by D.B.

The Clyde is a fascinating place and an everlasting source of interest to me. One of my jobs is to call on ships when they are in port for their requirements, to keep the office advised of progress of cargoes, repairs etc. Such visits are a great pleasure as there are always new things to be seen and discovered.

From Bromielaw to Clydebank there is an endless chain of

docks, slipways, cranes and derricks, a constant rattle of riveting and jackhammers, fires from welding torches or the blacksmiths braziers and scores of men swarming over the various jobs like ants. Ships on the move from berth to berth, going alongside to receive or discharge their cargoes with the dust telling the world this is a busy place.

So far I have not seen the pretty places of the Clyde. I believe the lower part of the river is really beautiful. What I have seen is the industrial section and I don't suppose one could call this section lovely, but it is inspiring and makes you feel that something is being done, something really creative.

I was present at a launching the other day, one of the big Cunarders took to the water at Clydebank, and it certainly was an impressive site. *Aquitania*, 45,674 tons; she was big enough to necessitate extra dredging to float her out and between the banks as the river is not very wide. When the chocks were knocked out she started down the ways quietly, sedately, like a lady, slowly meeting the river as her bulk gradually found the draft. Anchors were towing behind her to stop her speed as she went further in, would she stop in time or climb up on the opposite bank? But she was under complete control. With her bulk the water level rose and the spectators on the bank got a good wetting from the wash. She was then towed to the out-fitting birth. There she will receive her innards so to speak, come to life, to pulsate, to finally go down the river which gave her birth, to wander the wide oceans. A wonderful creation made from the bits and pieces put together by men's patience, ingenuity and labour.

Aquitania will follow in the wake of the first steamer built on the Clyde in 1812 which was the first steamer successfully operated in Europe. Built by Henry Bell her size was only twenty-eight tons. A monument to Henry Bell stands on the banks of the river at Dunglass, near Bowling.

My digs are near Charring Cross and the return fare from Charring Cross to St Vincent's Place where I work is a penny a day, which generally means a shilling a week. I must have mentioned this when writing home and my father passed it on to my grandfather, Lars. Lars had been a shoemaker all his life and had at one time employed a dozen men in his workshop. Now in his late sixties, he had more or less retired, although he kept his hand in with a small workshop at home. He had sired eighteen children of which my father was the eldest. There were children and grandchildren en masse, but I believe he always had a soft spot for me. So when he heard about me spending all that money on tram fares, he got down to his workbench and made me a most welcome pair of shoes, which he sent me and for which I was most grateful. Every time I took a tram ride, I felt guilty letting my grandfather down!

Of great interest were the rumblings from Germany and the Balkans. The slogan 'Drang nach Osten' (the quest to move towards the east) seemed to be on everyone's tongue. Tension was building up in Europe; King George V went on a goodwill tour of Germany to see his cousin, Kaiser Wilhelm II. Whether any good will resulted is a mute point, but the drift towards war continued and there is general apprehension of where the future was leading, and would England become involved?

It seems that so long as Germany's expansion proceeded along the lines laid down by Bismarck during the nineteenth century, meaning a land empire, a dominant army, a few colonies for purposes of exhibition rather than utility, then England would simply watch with that benevolence which she reserved for operations in which she was not a competitor. This attitude was slightly accentuated by a vague sense of kinship with Germany. After all, were not English kings and queens Germanic?

The historic fact is that since the Norman conquest in 1066, England's age-long tendency was to fight France, not the German states. But England had now become alarmed with German naval and overseas expansion, and felt she could no longer stand aloof from continental affairs. Indeed, the Kaiser with his erratic diplomacy and naval ambitions had pushed France and England together. In short, the Kaiser's behaviour had far more to do with England's support for France than any British taste for French society.

In addition, Ireland is also giving quite a deal of trouble to Mr Asquith (Prime Minister of England) so Hogmanay (New Year's Eve) 1914 was on a rising temperature and not a promising beginning for the new year, but the weather was glorious and the late spring and summer kept their promise.

On 28 June 1914, the Austrian Archduke Franz Ferdinand and his morganatic wife were assassinated in Sarajevo, Bosnia, by a student of Austrian-Hungarian nationality, a Slav nationalist, Gavrilo Princip. The Archduke had gone to Sarajevo to be present at some military manoeuvres and he and his wife were shot shortly after their arrival. Negotiations to localise the impact of the assassination were carried out in the hope that war may be averted. But this fond hope was to come to nothing.

I shall always remember 4 August. There were six of us, two students from the university, a business friend and two elderly ladies, who had converted the family mansion into a most comfortable boarding house in the quiet Hill End area. We had long ago finished dinner, were just talking about the prospects of war and how it would affect us. It was now midnight and Hill End was indeed a quiet place, a new suburb with few houses. Then suddenly a loud cry from a large crowd approaching the area and one of our friends called out, 'This is the war.'

Lord Kitchener had been appointed secretary of war and his stern face on posters is everywhere, with his dictum, 'Your country needs you.' It is a most dramatic and telling poster, a real bit of art, which will live in history after the present troubles fade and the memory of the heroes it depicts is forgotten. He immediately asked for 100,000 volunteers and got them.

I suppose at the beginning we were walking about with bated breath for events to happen. The navy quickly took command at sea. Action came quickly when on 9 August, HMS *Birmingham* sank the first German submarine. The naval battle of Heligoland on 28 August accounted for three German light cruisers, a destroyer and damaged a number of other ships. The British came away practically unscathed.

The Germans soon got their revenge. On 17 September the German submarine U-9 sank three British cruisers with the loss of 1,400 men. They were steaming in line abreast when HMS *Abouker* was hit and commenced to sink; her consorts went to her assistance to pick up survivors and were in turn torpedoed. It was a sad blow. The admiralty ordered that from now on heavy ships were not to pick up survivors.

The author's concept of his father's 'digs' in Glasgow.

CHAPTER 4

THE SHIPPING OFFICE

In spite of Britain being at war the work in the office is going on much as usual. There are a few more regulations to cope with and we are certainly busy. As can be expected shipping is being organised on a large scale, a lot of ships have been commandeered and taken over by various government instrumentalities. In a way, everything seems to be in a flux, but an orderly sort of flux. The Clyde is in perpetual motion and factories big and small are humming with activity day and night.

Had a letter from my father today who warns me to be ready to come home at short notice in case the war should spread and Norway becomes involved. The Norwegian merchant fleet is the danger point. German submarines have already attacked our ships and killed men. Norway, which has always been conspicuously anglophile, has given every sign that the Norwegian merchant fleet would continue to keep open the British trade routes and support their requirements to the fullest extent. The Norwegian attitude is very evident and it is surprising the Germans haven't protested.

We had chartered a Norwegian steamer of about 4500 tons with a cargo of grain (rice) from Mauritius to London and Glasgow. Half-way through the Suez Canal the skipper cabled that she had sprung a leak. They had not been able to discover where the leak was located, probably from rivet heads. As the leak was a slow one, they would be proceeding under usual speed, but would report if it showed signs of developing.

Successfully having avoided mines and submarines, she

arrived at Glasgow a few days later. When I went on board, the covers had been taken off the hatches and the grain was sprouting quite healthily through the cracks in the hatches. There was also an unpleasant, rotten smell; obviously the cargo had fermented. Unloading continued, and we looked for rivet holes; they were obviously the cause of the trouble. Some three to four days later the mate came to the office to report the unloading had been completed and she was empty.

'Well how is she?' I asked more about the rivet holes than anything else.

'How is she?' he said. 'She smells like a dead ship owner, and there is nothing meaner,' was his unfeeling sentiment.

This put me in mind of another skipper who described his attachment to his good ship in the following terms: 'Oh weal, she is an auld fat biddy, but a comfortable one.'

Another skipper who had just returned from a boisterous voyage summed his ship up as follows: 'She rolls like an atrocity; you would not believe what that girl was up to across the bay. She must have been conceived by a mad naval architect with a crooked line.' Evidently there were high steppers even among the tramp steamers!

It seems the land fighting is not going well. Conflicting rumours and unreliable information, plus willing gossipers make it difficult to sort out how things are really shaping. The Belgians were soon in difficulty and in spite of British marines and naval volunteers being sent to reinforce their defences, Antwerp fell on 10 October 1914.

At sea, things are not so encouraging either; the Battle of Coronel off the west coast of South America was a great disappointment and people were beginning to ask nasty questions.

The German raider *Emden* (Captain Karl von Muller) is in the meantime enjoying a charmed life, harassing the eastern sea routes, causing considerable damage. When she first entered the Indian Ocean, she very nearly ran into the British cruiser HMS *Hampshire* but missed out and made her appearance off the river Hooghly (near Calcutta). She ranged the Bay of Bengal and bombarded Madras on 22 September; then she cruised the waters off Ceylon, coaling at Diego Garcia (mid-Indian Ocean). On 21 October, again nearly running into the Hampshire and the armed merchant cruiser *Emperor of India*, she crossed to Penang, where she sank the Russian cruiser *Zhemchug* and the French destroyer *Mousquet*. Unfortunately, her store ship had been sunk by the *Yarmouth* and probably looking for her; she finally finished up at Cocos Island having sunk, in all, 23 allied ships without the loss of a single life.

Emden was the scourge of the shipping fraternity and her exploits were watched from hour to hour at the shipping exchange and at Lloyd's but nemesis was reaching out for her in the shape of the Australian cruiser HMS *Sydney* (Captain Glossop RN), who caught up with her at Cocos Island and in the ensuring battle completely destroyed her.

That was on 9 November 1914. I was at the Glasgow exchange when the news of her end was posted on the board about 11 am. I noticed members gathering around the board; then, there was sporadic cheering. I went over to see what it was all about. By that time the cheering was gathering force and they were all congratulating each other; many of them had suffered financially from the *Emden*'s plunders. But they didn't stay long; very soon the floor was empty; they had all gone to their favourite pubs or clubs to celebrate.

The end of the *Emden* was a much needed tonic after the Battle of Coronel where HMS *Good Hope* and *Monmouth* were sunk by von Spee's Pacific squadron on 1 November 1914 off the coast of Chile.

The Emden, known to her crew as the 'swan of the east', she was part of the Imperial Navy's prestigious China Squadron.

CHAPTER 5

GERMAN SURFACE RAIDERS

The remarkable achievements of the German light cruiser *Emden* in the Pacific and Indian oceans, thousands of miles from home, drew my attention to the place of 'surface raiders' in modern war. I found there was much more to it than simply the ad hoc sinking of merchant ships.

Towards the end of the nineteenth century, a stage was reached where the huge successes of German industry and scientific research, together with the inherent cultural values of the German people led the citizens of this relatively young central European empire to seek a greater share of world trade and a greater influence on world events. These sentiments were shared and encouraged by Kaiser Wilhelm II.

In contrast, England began to lose her previously undisputed position as the 'world's workshop'. By 1900, both the USA and Germany were producing more pig iron and steel than Britain. However, world markets were little affected at that time by the emergence of the USA as a leading industrial power since the rapid expansion of the American domestic market speedily mopped up her capacity to produce steel; this was not so with Germany. Her high quality steel products required a worldwide market.

Steel Output in Metric Tons

Date	UK	Germany
1880	3,730,000	1,548,000
1910	7,613,000	14,794,000

The aspiration of the German people at that time coincided with the belief that national power and prosperity depended upon overseas commerce, which in turn meant overseas possessions and influence. Unfortunately for Germany, Britain, France, Holland, Belgium and Portugal had already acquired the pick of overseas possessions.

In spite of the industrial advances in Germany and the USA, Britain's pre-eminence in world trade remained very evident. British shipping and British colonial trade was greater than that of France, Germany and the United States combined. Indeed both the prosperity and the comfort of Britain's citizens depended greatly on her pre-eminence in world trade and her merchant marine.

These facts were recognised by German naval planners; to them Britain's dependence on overseas trade could well be her Achilles heel; therefore, if war did eventuate with Britain, destruction of her overseas trade might prove decisive.

German planners never truly believed that the English people could be starved into submission by blockades, but believed that the combined efforts of the new German high seas fleet and worldwide surface raiders preying on merchant ships might destroy British shipping and trade, so as to force up food prices and damage commerce and industry due to a shortage of raw materials, so that a long suffering public would in time pressure the government to settle for a negotiated peace.

With these thoughts in mind, German naval planners set about devising a long term strategy, which in the event of war would all but destroy Britain's overseas trade.

During the period when the then 'great powers' were watching events in South Africa (i.e. Boer War), China (i.e. Boxer Uprising), the Balkans and the Middle East (Syria, Egypt, Palestine and Turkey), Germany was busily establishing naval bases in the Indian and Pacific Oceans and making friends with Turkey.

Germany, with the compliance of Turkey, constructed the eastern section of the Berlin to Baghdad railway (then part of the Ottoman Empire) and planned to extend the line to Kuwait at the northern end of the Persian Gulf. Plans were also made to establish a naval base on the Farasan Islands (owned by Turkey) at the southern end of the Red Sea.

These plans if brought to fruition could well stop ships utilising the

Suez Canal and allow German troops to be rapidly deployed to Kuwait and transported to India.

In the Pacific, Germany acquired possessions at Kiauchow Bay (i.e. Tsingtao or Quingdo) in North China, Micronesia, German Samoa and German New Guinea (Kaiser Wilhelmsland). Many of these possessions were regarded primarily as naval refuelling (bunkering) stations and were in fact administered by the Imperial Navy. In addition, Germany also acquired considerable political influence in Mexico and a number of South American states.

The operational plans for the Imperial German Navy for the Pacific and Indian Oceans, if and when war occurred with Britain, was to utilise these bases from which to attack merchant shipping and bombard specific ports so to be of such a threat that British ships would simply not leave port without adequate naval escorts. This would force Britain to relocate warships from the North Atlantic and by doing so, weaken Britain's home defences and anti-submarine capability.

In short, German surface raiders, both naval cruisers and armed merchant ships were to be an important part of German maritime strategy in the event of war with Great Britain.

In 1910 a detailed proposal was formulated to establish a naval base at Tsingtao and to station there a powerful squadron of ships including two new heavily armed cruisers (the *Scharnhorst* and *Gneisenau*) and three light cruisers including the *Emden*. This squadron was under the command of Vice Admiral Maximillian von Spee.

Many of these carefully laid plans were to be of no avail, for within weeks of declaring war, many of Germany's overseas bases were seized by the allies. Australian troops seized German New Guinea, New Zealand troops seized German Samoa and Japanese forces blockaded and seized Tsingtao. These moves forced von Spee to move his east Asiatic fleet from Tsingtao through the myriad of Germany's tiny island possessions to the west coast of South America. His intentions were now to harass shipping off the South American coast, then round Cape Horn, shell Port Stanley (British Falkland Islands), harass shipping in the South Atlantic and then attempt to breach the British blockade and return home to Germany. A very ambitious plan.

Spee was nevertheless a realist and has been quoted as saying, 'I am quite homeless; I must prowl the seas of the world doing as much mischief as I can until my ammunition is finished or a more powerful fleet succeeds in catching me.' These words were to prove prophetic. Von Spee utterly defeated a weaker British fleet off Coronel (Chile) just south of Valpariso (November 1914). He then rounded Cape Horn bound for the Falkland Islands where he was surprised by a superior British fleet. In the following battle, von Spee was utterly defeated and he, like most of his crew, drowned.

The loss of the *Emden* and von Spee's squadron effectively put an end to German naval presence in the Pacific, Indian and South Atlantic oceans. The British blockade of Germany made it very difficult for the Imperial German Navy to send out further ships to replace their losses and to harass allied shipping. U-boats whose operational range was limited by their fuel capacity were not an option for overseas operations.

In spite of these difficulties, the German navy did fit out a number of heavily armed and camouflaged converted freighters (e.g. the *Mowe* and *Wolf*), which did pass through the blockade and did sink British ships in the Pacific. But in general, British merchant ships in the Pacific and Indian Oceans were able to move freely.

To try and overcome these problems a German naval officer Count Felix von Luckner suggested fitting out a fast and innocent looking windjammer armed with hidden weapons and fitted with a 1000 horse power diesel engine for emergency use. Such a vessel would not need refuelling as it would depend mainly on its sails. Initially the German admiralty regarded the idea as ridiculous. The story goes that von Luckner remarked to the Kaiser, 'Well, your Majesty, if our admiralty says it is ridiculous, then I am sure it can be done, for the British admiralty will also think it ridiculous and they won't be on the look out for anything so absurd as a raider disguised as a harmless old sailing ship.' So the *Seeadler* (Sea Eagle) was born – a windjammer as a surface raider.

For 224 days the *Seeadler*, disguised as a Norwegian windjammer, prowled the south Atlantic and broad Pacific. She sank fourteen allied ships before running aground and breaking her back on a coral reef in the Society Islands, north east of New Zealand. All this had been achieved at the cost of one life. She was certainly a worthy successor of the *Emden*.

Certainly, German surface raiders had some striking successes but in reality they had little influence on the outcome of World War I. The superiority of the Royal Navy and Germany's lack of resources were to prove decisive.

References: Dr Peter Overlack, *Academic Exchange Scholarship* (Doctoral Thesis, University of Queensland).

Oliver E. Allen, *The Seafarers – The Windjammers* (Amsterdam, Time-Life Books).

Von Spee in the Pacific, 1914

PART THREE

CHAPTER 6

THE KAISER'S MOTHER

'History maketh a young man to be old without wrinkles or grey hair; privileging him with the experience of age without either the infirmities or inconveniences thereof.' – Fuller

'Vicky', eldest daughter of Queen Victoria.
She became Empress of Prussia and mother of Kaiser Wilhelm II.
(Wikipedia)

World War I and its aftermath was one of the greatest disasters of our age. The causes were multi-factorial but one of these causes was the erratic behaviour of the German Kaiser. This is the story of his mother and the tragic death of his father.

When Wilhelm I, emperor of the new German empire was crown prince of Prussia, he fell in love with a Polish princess, Elise Radziwill. The Prussian court, however, did not believe that a minor Polish aristocrat was an acceptable wife for a Prussian Hohenzollern and he was not allowed to marry her. He nevertheless pledged that he would never give his affection to anyone else.

Later and worse still, Wilhelm was ordered to propose to Princess Marie Louise Augusta of Saxe-Weimar, a German principality, and he dutifully did so. Augusta accepted with an equal lack of enthusiasm and they were married in 1829. It was, not surprisingly, an unhappy marriage, but they did have two children, a son Frederick Wilhelm (later Kaiser Frederick III) and a daughter Louise. As could be expected, these children had an unhappy childhood.

Queen Victoria of England (whose mother was German) married her cousin Albert of Saxe-Coburg-Gotha, another small German principality. Victoria and Albert, with their Germanic background, hoped to play a part in forging closer ties between the British Empire and Prussia (which was to become Germany), the rising force in Europe. Augusta, for her part, disliked the conservatism and militaristic ideas dominant in Prussia and admired the more liberal and constitutional British monarchy. It was therefore arranged for 'Vicky' (Queen Victoria's elder daughter, whose name was Victoria Adelaide Mary Louise, but to distinguished her from her famous mother was always 'Vicky') and the Crown Prince Frederick to meet. They not only met but were soon married. It proved to be a true love match, just as Victoria and Albert's was.

The Crown Prince and Vicky, unlike Frederick's father Wilhelm and his chancellor Bismarck, were a liberal and loving couple but unfortunately had to deal with a number of medical problems. Vicky had eight children. The eldest, Prince Wilhelm (later Kaiser Wilhelm II) came into the world via a difficult breach delivery, which resulted in a severe traction injury to the nerves supplying his left arm (Erb-Duchenne paralysis). This injury left Wilhelm with a partly paralysed and withered arm, which worried him throughout his life.

Vicky had three other boys and four girls. Two of the boys died at a young age, one of meningitis and one of diphtheria, although some writers claim that the diagnosis in those days was uncertain and that both boys may have had haemophilia, meaning Vicky was a carrier and had inherited the defective gene from her mother – this seems unlikely.

As harrowing and sad as were the deaths of two sons and the problems with Wilhelm's left arm, a greater and more politically damaging illness was to shorten the life of Vicky's beloved husband Frederick.

In January 1887, Frederick became hoarse and a small growth was noted on his left vocal cord, which was cauterised (a difficult procedure in 1887), but a recurrence was noted six months later. The German specialists diagnosed laryngeal cancer and advised removal of the larynx, a very major and, at that time, a potentially lethal procedure, which in 1887 would have had to be carried out with the patient having an open ether or chloroform anaesthetic in the presence of an already compromised airway and without the benefit of intravenous fluids, or blood and of course without any antibiotic cover.

Not unreasonably, Vicky insisted on another opinion and Dr Morell Mackenzie, an Englishman and at that time regarded as one of the greatest living authorities on diseases of the throat, was consulted. Mackenzie advised a biopsy before any such radical surgery, again not an unreasonable recommendation, but with the facilities available at that time it was not easy to obtain a true representative specimen. The biopsy was carried out and the tissue obtained was sent to the great German pathologist Virchow (the creator of cellular pathology). Virchow could not find any evidence of cancer in the tissue presented to him, so, in spite of protests from the German surgeons, laryngectomy was not carried out and probably at a time when the cancer was removable.

After the biopsy and seemingly good news, Frederick and Vicky went to England for three months and Queen Victoria knighted Mackenzie at the insistence of her daughter for 'saving' Frederick's life. Three months later Frederick lost his voice completely. The diagnosis was now obvious, Mackenzie changed his opinion but the cancer was now inoperable and Frederick began to suffocate. On 9 February 1888 a tracheotomy was carried out (a hole placed in his wind pipe and probably through cancerous tissue). A week later Frederick's father Wilhelm I, emperor of Germany, died aged ninety-one. Now unable to speak and too weak to attend his father's funeral, Frederick stood weeping at a palace window as the funeral procession passed by.

Frederick, now Emperor Frederick III of Germany, ruled for only eighty-eight days. He died a miserable death early on the morning of 15 June 1889.

Vicky was now a widow and not popular in Germany. The German specialists attending Frederick had been correct in their early diagnosis, Mackenzie had been wrong. Vicky, a liberal, had been against some of the expansionist policies of the new German empire, an unpopular point of view in Germany and she was well aware of the failings of her eldest son, now the new Emperor Wilhelm II. She realised sadly, that with Frederick's death, her father's and mother's dream of a liberalised Germany in partnership with England would also die.

Vicky was a well-educated and multilingual woman and at heart she was always English. Following the death of her beloved husband she went into semi-retirement but remained loyally in Germany. She had built a palatial country seat named Schloss Friedrichshof in the Taunus hills. She died of cancer in 1901, outliving her famous mother, whom she adored, by only eight months. She was interred next to her husband whom she had always loved, at the royal mausoleum of Friedenskirche at Potsdam.

Wilhelm II, the new Kaiser, was an ambitious, unstable and restless man. In his youth he had spent happy holidays in England, he even regarded himself as his grandmother, Queen Victoria's, favourite grandson. He developed an 'unhappy admiration' for the British Empire and the Royal Navy. He emulated the English aristocracy by taking part with great enthusiasm in sailing regattas at Cowes. He purchased and had yachts built specially to outsail his uncle's famous yacht *Britannia* and even set up the Kiel Yachting Regatta to emulate Cowes. Indeed he, as crown prince, had decided that when he became emperor, he too would have his overseas colonies and a great navy.

There were no doubt many causes for England going to war in Europe in 1914, but certainly the unstable personality of Kaiser Wilhelm II was one of those causes.

CHAPTER 7

The Beginning

'Many books have been written about the terrible innocence of these days; of a generation reared in peace, aching for the excitement of war.'
– James McMillan, *The Way It Was, 1914–1934*
(London, William Kimber, 1979)

At the outbreak of the First World War the whole world was dominated by nations of European stock and this included the United States, which in 1914 remained culturally still a part of Europe. The one exception to this generalisation was Japan.

The murder of Archduke Franz Ferdinand was certainly deplorable, but hardly fatal to world peace. Grand dukes had been murdered before and Serbia's attempts to prise the southern Slavic provinces from Austrian control had been a fact of life for so long that it scarcely roused interest in Europe. Nevertheless this murder set off a chain of events that lead five weeks later to The Great War.

The Habsburgs

The Habsburgs were once the greatest of sovereign dynasties of Europe. At the outbreak of World War I the ruling Habsburg was Franz Joseph, Emperor of Austria and King of Hungary. Francis Joseph, however, ruled over a very diverse empire, made up of Austrians, Germans, Czechs, Poles, Slovenians and Ruthenium's while Hungary incorporated Magyars, Rumanians, Slovaks and southern Slavs. To his credit he strove in the face of great difficulties to maintain harmony within his European empire.

Unfortunately, Franz Joseph also had to cope with a number of domestic tragedies. In 1867 his brother Maximillian who had been enticed to become Emperor of Mexico was shot by a firing squad. Next, his son Rudolph became mentally disturbed by the conflicting influences of an ultra-traditional father and a wilful and wayward mother. Rudolph shot himself and his young lover of seventeen days in 1889. Ten years later, the empress, Franz Joseph's wife, was stabbed to death by an anarchist, and finally, his nephew, and now heir to the throne, the Archduke Francis Ferdinand, was assassinated together with his morganatic wife in the Bosnian capital, Sarajevo, on 28 June 1914, setting in train events that led to the World War.

The Archduke Franz Ferdinand was as stupid as his cousin Rudolph, if not more so. He had an unhealthy passion for hunting. He scoured the globe for species to kill with a zeal that far exceeded the social demands of the day. Fascinated by the machine gun, he had forest animals driven into his sights for the kill. At his hunting lodge at Knopiste their bodies were stuffed and mounted under glass in their thousands. He was in fact responsible for bringing the European bison to the point of extinction. The assassination of this stupid man was perhaps a blessing to all wild life, but the nature of his killing initiated the slaughter of millions of human beings.

By midnight on 4 August, five weeks after the assassination of the Archduke, six empires were at war: the Austrian-Hungarian Empire against Serbia, the German Empire against France, Britain and Russia, the Russian Empire against Germany and Austria-Hungary and the Ottoman Empire against Russia, France and Britain.

Of all the European nations involved in The Great War, Britain was the most reluctant. The fear of Europe being dominated by Germany, the perceived threat posed by Germany's naval expansion and finally the German invasion of Belgium swung the liberal cabinet of Mr Asquith to ask the King-Emperor George V to sign the declaration of war with Germany.

Britain had never maintained a big army. Her regular army was a small professional, very well trained force, especially suited for such military encounters Britain might expect for the protection of her overseas dependencies and colonies. It was stated that the force available for all these pre-war commitments was about 160,000 men. So amidst those vast European armies filled by national systems of compulsory military service, the British alone in 1914 relied on a purely voluntary professional army (conscription was introduced in England in 1916).

Kitchener Needs You!
War minister Lord Kitchener's famous recruitment poster was
quite unnecessary at this point – young men were flocking to the

*War minister, Lord Kitchener's famous recruitment poster was quite
unnecessary at this point – young men were flocking to the colours.*

When the war broke out in August 1914 the initial reaction was, 'It will be all over by Christmas.' That hopeful optimism was now beginning to fade and replaced by a more realistic appreciation that we were now dealing with a great war, involving tremendous forces, and now that it has got under way, it will not readily blow over.

On August 6 1914 the British cabinet discussed whether this army, altogether only six divisions, should be sent to France at all. In the end and on the advice of Kitchener, four divisions were sent across the channel. This was the British Expedition Force or BEF made up of a purely professional force of regulars. At the very beginning, the British contribution to the European struggle could only be a relatively small one compared with more than three million Austro-Hungarians, four million Frenchmen, 4,500,000 Germans and nearly six million Russians.

When Kitchener became War Minister, he predicted a long war, contrary to many government and military authorities. He demanded more men, more equipment and more materials. The people responded grandly to his call and by the end of the year a million men had enlisted. With territorials and other forces Britain had some two million men under arms.

At the outset Germany was faced with a war on two fronts, the Russian and French. Her plan was to quickly knock out France in the west and then with equal rapidity, knock out Russia in the east. This plan almost succeeded but not quite. The German advance into France through Belgium was only halted a few dozen miles north east of Paris on the river Marne, but it was halted and only six weeks after war had been declared. The Germans then withdrew to the north and both sides improvised parallel lines of defensive trenches and fortification, which stretched from Nieuport on the channel coast in Flanders 470 miles to the Swiss frontiers. This was the western front, which became a machine for massacre; it lasted for over four years.

Wilhelm II of Germany with Franz Joseph of Austria-Hungary

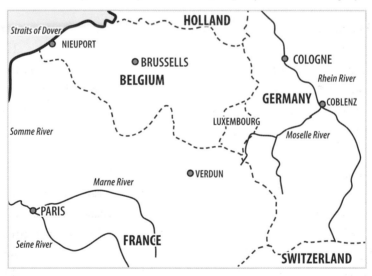

The author's map of Germany's western front, winter 1914 until summer
1918. The front extended from Nieuport on the Belgian coast to the Swiss
frontier and varied little over four years. It proved to be a human abattoir.
At Verdun, February to July 1916, there were 700,000 casualties. One
hundred and fifty thousand dead were left unburied to simply rot where they
fell. At the Somme, July to November 1916, there were 1,250,000 casualties.

Lieutenant Archer-Shee

(The Winslow Boy)

In 1908 George Archer-Shee, aged thirteen, a new cadet at Osborne Naval College, was expelled for allegedly cashing a five shilling money order that did not belong to him. His father, a retired Liverpool bank manager, believed his son was innocent and challenged the accusation.

It took two years before the case was resolved and the accused George Archer-Shee was completely exonerated. He had of course left the navy but in 1914, at the outbreak of war, he immediately enlisted in the army, was commissioned Lieutenant and posted to the South Staffordshire regiment.

The case involving Archer-Shee was raised in parliament and at one stage was compared to that of Captain Alfred Dreyfus of the French Army, who had been wrongly convicted of treason in 1894. Dreyfus, after spending years on the French penal colony of Devil's Island (Île du Diable), was found to be innocent and re-instated into the French Army where he served with some distinction during World War I and was subsequently awarded the Legion of Honour.

Lieutenant Archer-Shee was not so fortunate. Although he was not sent to a penal colony prior to his pardon, he sadly had the dubious distinction of being the first voluntary British officer to be killed in France during World War I (Ypres October 1914). He later became the central figure in Terence Rattigan's book *The Winslow Boy.*

References: James McMillan, *The Way It Was, 1914–1934* (London, William Kimber, 1979).
Martin Gilbert, *The First World War* (London, Harper Collins, 1994).

George Archer Shee, aged 13, as a cadet at Osbourne Naval College, seen with this father

PART FOUR

FRANCE, 1915

CHAPTER 8

Nantes

We admired the gyrations of the destroyer
as she buried her bow in the huge seas.

I have now been in Scotland nearly two and a half years and I began considering either returning home or finding 'another paddock' for my further apprenticeship. As luck would have it I came across an ad in Lloyd's *List and Shipping Gazette* offering a position with a French shipbroker's office in Nantes, which I thought might suit me. I replied by cable and after a short correspondence, I was offered the job.

I should mention that my original plan was to spend about two years in Great Britain, then another two years in Germany. But of course the war had paid full stop to this plan. France was certainly a good substitute; the only snag was that my French was poor. I had done some at the Athenaeum in Glasgow, especially since the Belgian refugees had arrived, but it was sketchy. Nevertheless I was there to learn.

I started my rounds of farewells and was quite surprised to find the number of friends I had made in the time I had been in Glasgow.

I went to the last musical evening at the Norwegian church and said goodbye to Mr and Mrs Meier. I left my cards at the club, had morning tea at the Exchange and finally a session with the staff, which of course became slightly hilarious. Miss Dewar produced high tea at her flat, and I came away feeling sorry to leave. In fact I had become very attached to Scotland, the people and even Glasgow, which so often has been named a dirty, ugly city.

I left on the *Argosy*, a 3100 ton tramp. She had been consigned to us for munitions and as I knew she was going to Nantes, I approached the captain for a free ride.

'Sure, come with us and be blown up,' was his ready offer.

We left on a nice sunny day in May, but it blew like stink once we got outside. *Argosy* was a typical, short-voyage tramp, known as the Three Islands type, a fo'c'sle, bridge and poop. It became very rough and the welldecks were continually submerged up to midships. The crew, who lived in the fo'c'sle, were unable to cross the deck and arrangements had to be made for them to bunk amidships. Quarters became cramped, but that was the only alternative. *Argosy* was behaving like a diving machine; her foredeck was constantly flooding, her fo'c'sle sticking out of the swirling seas like a spring-tide rock.

With the pounding she took, the cargo shifted and *Argosy* took a fifteen degree list to port, which was not good in that sea. The cargo consisted of shell casings, which were heavy machined tubes, about eight to ten feet long, like piping. They were ready-made to be cut up in sections and made into shell casings. They were heavy and, although securely stowed and battened down with ropes and chains, they nevertheless started to move. The bulk of the cargo was in the bottom of the ship and was secure, but part of the shell casings were stowed in the tween decks to counteract any pendulum effect on the ship's stability due to too much weight below. The tween deck cargo was now loose and should some of it get adrift and start sliding from side to side, it could easily go through the ship's side. So the mate and some of the men went into the tween decks to grapple with the wild, round steel casings, whilst the ship did its best to throw them all over the place. It was dangerous work, but they managed to tame the runaways.

The mate's comment when he came up, sweaty and dirty, was, 'When I return back to Blighty I shall get myself a small farm, as far away as possible from salt water and lousy steamers.'

But there was nothing wrong with the ship itself. *Argosy* was a well found ship for those days, no frills and flounces, but useful. Her speed was the usual ten knots, burning coal, but her ten knots were considerably reduced by half or less, when the weather turned nasty. Her accommodation was spartan: the usual galley amidships; a small mess room for the officers with a small cabin on either side; the captain's saloon above, small but also with two cabins, one of which was the captain's, the other being occupied by me; then a small chart-house on top with an open narrow railed-off bridge, which held the engine-room telegraphs. An awning was stretched halfway across the bridge in case it should rain. The maxim in those days was: 'Open bridge, so the helmsman and officer on watch won't go to sleep.'

When arriving at Land's End, a destroyer, who evidently knew all about us, signalled for us to proceed. She was to escort us to St Nazaire. So across the Channel and Bay of Biscay we rolled, admiring the gyrations of the destroyer as she buried her bow in the huge seas.

St Nazaire

The Loire is France's longest river and down through the years, vineyards, towns and lovely chateaux have grown up along its banks.

During the 1860s, Napoleon III, riding the crest of nationalistic fervour, after the successful conclusion of the Crimean War was determined to re-establish the French Merchant Marine. So the company Transat (later The French Line) was established with a hefty government grant and began operations from Le Havre at the mouth of the Seine River.

Transat initially purchased foreign-built ships and set up a trans-Atlantic service to America, Mexico and the Caribbean. But French pride dictated that ships carrying the French flag should be built in France. As a result the ship-building firm of Chantier de Penhoet was formed and located at St Nazaire at the mouth of the Loire, a more suitable location for ship-building. It was here that all of France's great liners were built, culminating in the magnificent *Normandy* who made her maiden voyage to New York in June 1935, breaking the trans-Atlantic record and earning the coveted blue ribbon.

These great French liners were owned by the French Line, which had long since replaced Transat. The French Line's home port was Le Havre but all their ships were built at St Nazaire.

Many years later the huge Cunard liner *Queen Mary II* was built at St Nazaire at a cost of $US1 billion. At 148,528 gross tonnes, she is twice the size of the *Normandy*.

We arrived at St Nazaire late at night and anchored for the pilot. He took us up the River Loire at early dawn and some hours later we tied up at the wharf, in the shadow of the Castle of Nantes.

Nantes is a shipping town located sixty kilometres upstream from the mouth of the Loire River and the large shipyards at St Nazaire.

I went ashore with Captain Sutton, who had been to Nantes before with his ship; in fact, my new office had been his agent for some time. I met Raymond Moser, my colleague, and I had my first briefing of conditions in my new job, somewhat different to what I had come from.

Moser, about my own age, hails from Alsace where his father has a rubber factory, which he was never allowed to forget. He was due for military service and liable for call up at any time. He was a delightful chap, clever, spoke good English and we became great pals. He did a lot to make my early days in Nantes easy.

M Goupil, head of the firm, arrived a little later, a spare little fellow with gold pince-nez and a slightly fussy manner, but pleasant, and gave me a hearty welcome to his city. I was later to learn that he is shockingly hen-pecked by a tiny wife with flaming red hair and green eyes; she had once been on the stage, and I believe she still thought she was.

I had my first encounter in halting French with the cashier, Mrs Goupil's niece, who giggled, which incidentally she did till the day I left. She was a long string bean of a person but happy and bright even when she giggled.

It was a small office so far as staff went, but as we were the authorised brokers for British, Norwegian and Portuguese vessels, and those were by far the most numerous ships using the port from overseas. We also undertook a fair amount of ship chartering, which meant a very busy office.

The port itself was interesting, with its broad river splitting the town in two. There was a considerable ship-building and repair establishment on one side of the river. The wharves were old, but good with plenty of warehouses. There were unfortunately shoals in the river, which had the nasty habit of shifting, so pilotage was compulsory for ships steaming up the Loire River from St Nazaire.

Nantes is a historical city with a population at that time of about 200,000 people. It was the chief town in the area even before the Roman conquest, and became a great commercial and administrative centre during their occupation.

One of the more historical events was the signing of the Edict of Nantes in 1598 by Henry IV of France, which granted some of his subjects, the Protestants who were Huguenots, a great measure of freedom. Incidentally, the edict was actually signed in our building. 'Edict of Nantes' is sculptured above the main entrance.

The main street, Quai de la Fosse, runs the full length of the main town parallel to the river and past the old castle. It was a typical cobblestone road, a salty thoroughfare of chandlers' shops, butchers, bakers, brothels and wine shops, with wharves and warehouses on the other or river side.

The traffic was still the old type horse drawn dray, although a few motor trucks and cars had made their hesitant entry. When the summer brought the warmth, the boys swam the river and as there was always a fair amount of current, the water was kept reasonably clear of today's curse, pollution.

On Sundays or holidays, the wharves were festooned with hundreds of fishing rods, with optimistic anglers patiently spending hours in the hope of bringing something home for supper. Out of curiosity I have watched them and would estimate that for every fifty dangling hooks, the catch would amount to one six-inch sardine, and when one was caught, it was jubilation all along the line of fishermen, and the catcher was, for the moment, the great hero.

In the meantime the war is gaining in momentum. The fighting in the Dardanelles has developed into a complete and bloody war, with a great deal of men and ships being involved without encouraging progress being shown. More troops are being sent and ships are constantly on the move, while the troops are battling the unfriendly terrain. The Turks in the meantime have been able to improve fortifications and reinforce their army.

On the other side of the Atlantic there are serious anti-German feelings, mostly caused by the submarine sinkings. Germany declared in February 1915 they would sink all surface vessels at sight, within a certain zone around Britain. To this President Wilson replied with a sharp protest stating that the USA would hold Germany accountable for any loss of life or property. When the British liner *Lusitania* was sunk in May with the loss of 1200 lives of which 128 were American, the general feeling in the States brought the crisis to near breaking point. When a French vessel, the *Sussex*, suffered a similar fate, also with American loss of lives, Wilson sent a strong protest to Germany resulting in Germany promising that in future submarines would issue a warning before firing a torpedo. This all seemed a little unrealistic to me. How could one expect a submarine to surface and expose itself before firing a torpedo at a fast moving liner? Nevertheless, I feel the writing is on the wall; sooner or later the USA will join the allies in the struggle.

I have decided to take French lessons and Yvonne (the giggler) has recommended her old school teacher, sixty-year-old Madame Sophie; she is no beauty but an excellent teacher.

I was not happy with the accommodation Raymond arranged for us; it was a family home and my room was on the second floor with one large window looking out and across a narrow lane to an identical house with an identical window, no more than twenty feet away.

The room opposite was occupied by two prostitutes who did most of their trade in hotel rooms but occasionally brought clients to their room. As blinds and curtains were not in use I was treated to some very erotic exhibitions. I learnt a great deal; *Le Grand Nie* par excellence.

After a while I was able to make Raymond realise that we ought to do better and we moved to more respectable and quiet surroundings. We settled in and acquired a housekeeper to cook for us. She proved to be a good cook, a very patient soul who accepted our bachelor habits and always produced something for the table when required. Madame Doucet, for that was her name, was a widow of generous good humour and ample proportions, served us well and made our establishment comfortable and pleasant.

The Cathedral at Nantes by Camille Corot

France, 1915

CHAPTER 9

Captain Bullock

In M Goupil's office, an exceedingly peaceful atmosphere reigned that sunny morning as we settled down to cope with our modest part of the world trade. We had gone through the morning's cables, when my colleague Raymond reminded me that SS *Gladiator* had not yet turned up. She was a 3000 ton steamship, having left Cardiff five days before with a cargo of coal.

Five days from Cardiff is longer than even the lowliest of tramps should take and *Gladiator* was not a lowly tramp, at least not by the standards of those days. We had not previously handled her, but we had arranged her charter on the basis of her plans and particulars, which showed her as a typical short voyage cargo vessel eminently suitable for the coal trade. Her speed was given at ten and a half knots so there was some reason for anxiety about her whereabouts. It was wartime and we thought she might have been held up by a naval patrol or even encountered a German submarine. There had been no bad weather, and as submarine sinkings at that time had been few and far between on this route, we decided to give her another day before cabling her owners.

In the meantime I got in touch with the Loire pilot station where I elicited the information that no vessel with that name had entered the river that morning.

'Mais parbleu', spat the garrulous pilot into the phone, 'un sacre, Capitaine d'un bateau,' he went on to tell me he had nearly run the pilot cutter down that morning, and refused to take him on board when he came alongside. The ship had gone for the mouth of the river at full speed and left the pilot wallowing in her wake. 'Je ne sais pas son nom mais sacrebleu il faut payer.'

I rang off knowing full well that hell holds no fury like a rejected pilot, especially if that pilot happens to be a full-blooded Briton. This seemed to me so much misplaced humour, as the river pilotage being compulsory, the pilot would get his fee anyway, whether the ship employed him or not. This is general practice in France.

Now and again a skipper would happen along that did not know of these regulations and did not realise that there were dangers of shifting sand bars and uncertain tides along the Loire. Some made it without mishap, but most without the help of a pilot ended up with their ship getting stuck on a shoal where she would remain until the next tide or until we could get a tug down to pull her off. In any case the result was always the same; we had to smooth the tempers of irate pilots who could only see in the skipper's independence a terrible slight on their profession. A task which was not made any easier if the skipper happened to be one of those stubborn self-opinionated gentlemen who thinks every landlover and shore based pilot is out to rob him.

I was musing on this later in the day, when in walked a rather greasy individual in a cheap reach-me-down dark suit.

A man of about thirty-five, medium build, with oily dark hair and moustache, not too clean looking; in fact the dark hair and moustache seemed not to belong and gave him a sallow complexion that somehow wasn't right. At first I took him for a fireman looking for his skipper, a logical conclusion which was soon dispelled.

'Is this Goupil's office?' he asked.

I said, 'Yes, this is Goupil's office and what can I do for you?'

'I am Captain Bullock of the *Gladiator*; here are my papers, and where is the nearest whore-house?'

With this, he threw down onto the desk a black satchel. I looked up in astonishment at this extraordinary introduction. However, having so to speak, acquired a fairly intimate knowledge of the various men who seek their livelihood on the wide oceans, I was not shocked. I took his greeting more as a clumsy, humorously meant salutation, so I merely brushed aside his request for directions to a brothel and tried to get down to business. 'How do you do, Captain Bullock? We have been rather worried about you; you are a couple of days overdue.'

'Oh hell, I was held up at Land's End by a ruddy destroyer who kept us hanging around for thirty-six hours. He said there was a submarine somewhere about and wouldn't let us proceed. Here are my papers; I'm alongside the consignees' wharf and starting discharging. Let me have twenty-five francs and tell me where I can find the nearest brothel.'

I had in the meantime looked at his papers, which were all in order. He had even drafted his cables to his owners, as well as to the shippers in Cardiff, informing them of his probable return for the next cargo. He had been chartered for ten consecutive voyages through us, and I expected to see a great deal of him during the coming three months. I was glad to note this, but his evident hankering after dames did not promise well. Brothels, booze and brawls generally go together and a ship master who deliberately sets a course for this kind of entertainment in the middle of a sunny afternoon can only be looked upon as a source of trouble and worry.

'These are alright,' I said looking up from his papers, 'and what about having a bit of lunch with me today?'

'No thank you,' came his prompt reply. 'All I want is a room with a girl.'

It was obvious that something was required of me; it was expected that my human kindness and understanding of a sailor's need should put him on the right track for his immediate needs.

A shipping office is undoubtedly the most comprehensive universal provider of jobs for its staff. In time we acquire a readiness to cope with all sorts of situations and requests unthinkable in any other business; but damn it all, it was decidedly not my duty to steer this salty hunk of passion on his amorous pursuit. Why the devil couldn't he be a reasonable being and like so many of his brother wanderers take his fun where he could find it in the more salubrious and certainly safer atmosphere of the numerous cafés and restaurants up town, which were generally crawling with women on the loose in the evenings, especially during wartime.

'Well,' I temporised, 'I cannot tell you much about whore houses. Anyhow, this is an odd time of the day to chase the girls. But if you go along in the evening to any of the cafés that line the streets you will have no difficulty in finding a partner for your night's frolics.'

'Hell with those,' he retorted. 'I don't want any demi-mondaine; I want a plain honest to goodness whore house with plenty of girls and no frills.'

The situation was certainly beyond me. The very ludicrousness of it struck me and I saw in my mind's eye, the skipper wandering down Quai de la Fosse in search of the red light district at a time when respectable citizens are easing up a bit on the morning's work and wondering what the missus will be preparing for his midday meal and I tried to picture the kind of reception that he would receive from a household of damsels who probably had not yet been able to shake off their efforts of the previous night. They certainly wouldn't be very glamorous at that time of day, I burst out laughing.

'I say, Captain, you couldn't possibly mean that; you, a ship's master, who knows what these places are like; you have often enough seen what damage they can do.'

My laughter met with a warm smile, or perhaps it was a grin, a happy go lucky kind of grin; his face relaxed, there was a sparkle of unexpected friendliness in his eyes. Somehow my laughter had touched a cord and brought forward a spontaneous response but it lasted for a moment only, then it was wiped and he stalked out.

'I know alright,' he flung back at me.

Well, well, I thought, it's your business if you get a broken head or worse but what will you do without money? In his hurry he had forgotten the twenty-five francs he had asked for so I half expected him back again. Instead of which the morning's work was effectively interrupted by the arrival of Monsieur Lefevre, the senior pilot in charge of the port office, his ever open overcoat, which he wore at all seasons, billowing out like an Arab tent on the collapse.

Capitaine Lefevre, as he was better known, was a bit of a character and a wonderful raconteur. He went to sea in his youth and tasted the hardships and the glories of that period when sailing ships held the seafaring stage before they faded away. But it was mostly of the glories he would tell, for although he may at times appear rather overpowering, he was human enough with a sense of romance to spin his yarns without dwelling over much of the dreary parts of those days.

But it was not to while away an idle moment that he came this sunny morning; far from it, his eyes were flashing and his chubby hands were fanning the air as he confirmed the suspicion I had nourished all morning, that it was the *Gladiator* which had refused to take his colleague on board; more, she had nearly run him down and certainly half filled his gig with very cold salt water. The sad tale, beautifully embroidered, of course, had been phoned through to him from the pilot station and by the simple process of elimination it had not taken him long to trace the crime to *Gladiator*. He had promptly proceeded on board to have it out with the skipper, but as that gentleman was away on pleasure bent, had cornered the chief officer who could only admit the incident. His entire being exuded a righteous temper at the indignity that his friend had been subjected to; not only had he been insulted and treated like a pirate instead of a pilot, Captain Lefevre and the entire pilot service, if not the whole Republic of France, of which the pilot service was part, were smarting under this incredible affront. 'Sacré nom de nom, c'est un outrage. Un gros outrage!'

So once more did I admire the technique of unparalleled verbosity by an expert. I was truly spellbound by the oration, by the verve, which lifted the performance to its highest level of perfection, that truth to tell I did not so much listen to what he had to say as to watch with awe the animated spectacle he presented.

Steam having been let off, it was a comparatively easy matter to smooth away the last simmerings of temper and when I suggested it was time for an apéritif, he linked his arm in mine and we left the office with the disapproval of M Goupil who had on previous occasions expressed his dislike for people who wore vile ties and smoked sour cigars.

Madame Rollins' Café des Arts was one of several wine shops lining Quai de la Fosse. It was one of the quieter ones and had become the rendezvous of the waterfront. Here came shipping men, charterers, ship masters, officers, consignees and stevedore foremen. Pilots drifted in, tugboat masters came in search of captains. It was a cosmopolitan crowd who spoke a variety of languages. By and large, Madame Rollins' establishment was becoming a shipping exchange, a twentieth-century Lloyd's coffee house.

'Bonjour, Monsieur le Capitaine. Bonjour, Monsieur Edmond.' (Edmond was my father's nickname, and I am unsure how I acquired it). She answered our greetings as we entered and ordered our Dubonnets. A couple of skippers were at a table, inviting each other for lunch and having difficulty in deciding on whose vessel the hospitality should be enjoyed. Madame Rollins came to our table to show us the latest photograph of her two young daughters, Yvonne and Suzanne, taken at Yvonne's tenth birthday.

Madame Rollins was a good looking capable woman, somewhere in her early thirties, of satisfying contours and healthy colour. She gazed charmingly at you out of a pair of china blue eyes, rather rare in that part of the world. She never got ruffled. I have never seen her put out, not even by misguided guests, who when the wine fired their amours, forgot their manners and became obviously too friendly. On these occasions she would say, 'Eh bien, Monsieur,' with just the intonation that made the unfortunate squirm and betake himself elsewhere. She was a good woman, a faithful wife to her husband who at the time was fighting the Boche (German), lice and rats within the perimeter of Verdun. She looked after their two daughters in the most admirable though typical French fashion, and I am sure she ran the café most efficiently on her own. She had common sense and, as with most French women, an inborn instinct to make a profit.

Many a client had reason to be thankful to Madame Rollins. If it should happen that the day had been long, the conviviality on such a generous scale and with the approach to 'lights out' found you well and truly up to the scuppers, Madame Rollins was not the one to shoo you out into a dark, cold world. Especially the cold, dark world of the Quai de la Fosse. On the contrary, you would be ushered along to a small billiard room at the back, where Madame would make you quite comfortable on one of the billiard tables with pillows etc. kept for the purpose in a little locker in the corner.

Now she was telling us about her two daughters; how Suzanne was the favourite with the Mother Superior of her school and Yvonne was growing so tall that her frocks always had to be lengthened. How her poor husband had written three months ago that he would soon get leave and yesterday she received news from him that all leave had been stopped. 'But he will come soon,' she bravely adds. 'No, thank you, I won't have a sherry today. J'ai la migraine,' she sighs ever so perceptively and goes back to her desk.

A little later and after we had settled down I was intrigued to learn from Lefevre that Captain Bullock came from well to do people and that he had had the benefit of a good education. Somehow I had failed to fix him as a backslider, the black sheep of the family.

The following afternoon, Captain Bullock came to the office, stating his vessel would be discharged during the night and he intended to leave at daybreak. Were his papers ready? I had them all there in his black satchel with copies of his cables, time sheets etc. Would he please fill them in with the exact time of completion of discharge and hand it to the pilot we had ordered for him, so that he could bring them back to us? 'Right,' was his only comment as he picked up the satchel.

I looked at him and wondered at his offhandedness. A devil must have prompted me or perhaps it was merely pique, produced by my inability to classify this strange skipper, so I could not help asking him if he had found his houses of whores to his liking.

'Oh rather,' was his curt rejoinder. 'A bloody fine place, good food, real coffee, and all for ten francs.'

Swagger, I thought and rashly invited him for dinner.

'No thank you,' he unhesitatingly answered. 'I am going back to the ship now to see everything is in order.' And once more he turned on his heels and stalked out without even proffering the usual goodbye of a captain to his agent.

The *Gladiator* made a quick return trip and was back with

a fresh cargo in nine days. He appeared at the office with his papers, then disappeared until he came to fetch them again for his departure. This continued, voyage after voyage, performed regularly without any fuss or bother. Apart from these two visits to the office each voyage, we did not see Captain Bullock. He never appeared at Café des Arts, nor at any other place where ships' officers usually meet to compare notes. On one or two occasions when his rare visit to the office coincided with the presence of other ship masters, I did my best at introductions, but his attitude was so unresponsive as to border on rudeness that I decided never again. He was a loner who had his own idea of how to spend his time in port. But so far as the business of his ship and the charter was concerned, everything went very satisfactorily, so much so that we renewed the charter for another ten voyages.

He had been running for us for some two or three months when he suddenly came back from Cardiff a very changed man. At first I could hardly recognise him. Gone was his black hair and moustache; now he was clean shaven and his head was crowned with a fine crop of wavy, steel-grey hair. The sallow complexion had disappeared; so had the shabby reach-me-down; he now sported a smart grey tweed. He was a good looking respectable gentleman, prematurely grey but still with the vigour of healthy manhood showing in his bearing. It was difficult to recognise in him the grubby, oily individual I had become accustomed to. He saw my surprise, curbed that winning smile I could sense lurking ready to break through, and explained defiantly, 'I used to dye my hair and moustache, but have decided to do without from now on.'

'I hope you will never change that decision,' I replied. 'You are a different man. Perhaps you can find time to have lunch with me?' Rather an ungracious way of extending an invitation perhaps, but to my surprise he accepted after a moment's hesitation.

Our housekeeping was run on a conveniently elastic basis as we kept fairly open house for friends and intimates. It was not unusual to arrive home and find the table set for six or eight instead of for just our two selves. It was an unwritten law between us that we did not bother to inform each other if we were bringing guests along; we only phoned Madame Doucet to put more 'water in the soup'.

Captain Bullock and I were the first to arrive. Madame told us that Raymond was also bringing a guest, so that the table was set for four. Bullock had been very quiet during our short walk home. His contribution to the conversation had been purely monosyllabic; now he closed up completely. The fact that he was to meet two other strangers and sit at table with them seemed to completely unnerve him.

We were in the sitting room having the usual apéritif when I heard Raymond arriving with his guest. It was Captain Lefevre. Oh, yes, it was Lefevre alright; there was no mistaking his gallant greetings of Madame Doucet. Bullock had never met Lefevre, so far as I knew, and it would be interesting to note Lefevre's reactions at being introduced to one of the blackest sinners against the code of the sacred pilot service.

But I could have spared myself these speculations, because on entering and discovering who was there, Lefevre opened his arms in the really exuberant French fashion and with an 'Ah, mon cher Capitaine,' it looked as if he was going to embrace and kiss the embarrassed skipper. However, it did not come to that; but it was very apparent that they were close friends and their friendship must have been of a long standing as they addressed each other by their Christian names. It was also evident that they had met recently. I did not voice any surprise at discovering their friendship. I was mostly watching Bullock, whose French was good, and it was pleasant to note that his nervousness melted under the flow of comradeship that Lefevre poured forth. I was soon to learn much more about Captain Bullock.

CHAPTER 10

LEFEVRE'S STORY

A couple of days later I ran into Lefevre outside Brasserie Moderne and asked him in for a drink. The place was fairly empty but slowly filling with the usual clientele of men, old and young, idling away the evening, ogling the women, who, practically without exception, led that peculiar twilight existence of the oldest profession without actually being street-walkers. They were mostly mistresses whose men had been mobilised and sent to the front.

These women were bored to distraction and more than willing to accept a drink, accompany you to a show or a meal and, if your desires went so far, she might allow you to spend the night in her apartment while her 'ami' was at the front and whose pay provided the rent. All very simple and convenient.

We found a quiet corner table and with the drinks before us, I opened the conversation by expressing pleasure at his friendship with Captain Bullock, especially as it was not so long ago he had consigned him to everlasting perdition.

'Oh that was nothing, just a little mistake. Jimmy is a grand fellow. Il est un brave homme, yes, mon cher, he is one of the bravest men alive today. But I suppose you know all about that?'

I assured him I new nothing about 'that' whatsoever. On the contrary, I knew very little about Captain Bullock.

I described to him my unfavourable first impression and then my surprise and pleasure to find him so greatly changed when he recently returned from Cardiff.

'Yes, Jimmy is a funny chap,' Lefevre continued, 'He is a big school boy at heart and will always remain so. When I met him on the Quai de la Fosse I hardly recognised the man I knew and admired four years ago. Monsieur Edmond, I admire him more than our Joffre and Foche; they are both very clever and will save our country from the Boche but they get other men to do the dangerous jobs. Jimmy is both brave and very courageous.'

The restaurant was fairly full now and the waiters had a busy time. A brace of pretty girls sat down at the next table and threw us inviting glances but it was a wasted effort as Lefevre continued.

'Four years ago the Norwegian oil tanker *Odin*, bound for Gibraltar with a full cargo of oil, was 130 miles north of Madeira, steaming her steady twelve knots across a glassy sea under a blue sky.

'She was a fine staunch vessel having been completed about twelve months previously and carried a little over 8000 tons of oil in her tanks. There was a slight swell, a long roll coming up astern making her dip her sharp bow sufficiently to turn the hiss of her cutwater into a burbling chant, rising or falling a few notes with the plunge or upward heave of her forebody. That, and the thump, thump of pistons in the engine room were the only sounds to break the sleepy peace of the afternoon. A thin wisp of smoke from the oil burning furnaces issued from her funnel and drifted out over her wake; then suddenly, this calm and peaceful scene was shattered in the early evening when a huge flame shot up from the *Odin*. I have never been able to ascertain exactly what happened aboard the *Odin*, neither the cause of the fire nor the sequence of events. Yet, it is fairly certain that the fire started in one of the forward tanks, and although they immediately put into action their fire-fighting appliances, it spread with shocking rapidity. The engines were stopped to prevent the speed-made wind from fanning the flames into greater fury and in the forlorn hope of preventing them extending aft. All these efforts were of no avail.

'Soon, explosions were heard when the heat and pressure burst open manholes, pipes and bulkheads, smaller explosions like rifle shots occurred when rivets were forced out of decks, hatches and hull. Burning oil flowed through these openings and enveloped the ship in a veritable sea of flames. All this happened with unbelievable speed. The transformation of a fine ship to a burning inferno took less than a minute.

'Immediately the fire was discovered, the master broadcast an urgent SOS to all vessels within range. The wireless operator stood by his post till the set went dead on him, receiving answers and giving fresh information.

'The British trader *Warrior* was on a voyage to the Grand Canaries. She was Jimmy Bullock's first command, although it was not his first voyage as master. She was *Gladiator*'s predecessor, very much the same type, and is still running, unless the Boche has got her during the last four or five days. Her owners were employing her on the regular cargo trade between England, the Bay of Biscay the Iberian Peninsula, Madeira and the Canaries. I was a passenger – really a guest – the one and only passenger, on my way to visit my married sister in Madeira. During the eight days I had been on board, I had come to know and like Jimmy as I have liked few people. It was soon evident to me that in spite of his youth he was a first rate skipper and a fine sailor. So although he may have obtained his appointment by virtue of being the owner's nephew, he was fully worthy of it and the trust they had put in him, I knew, would never be betrayed.

'He is still a young man but he was four years younger then, when he was suddenly called upon to handle a situation as hopeless and difficult as it is possible to imagine.

'*Warrior* was the nearest vessel to receive the SOS. She was less than an hour's steaming away. As a matter of fact, while Sparks (wireless operator) was receiving the message, the skipper and his second mate were on the bridge wondering at the fierce glow that shot up from below the horizon, lighting up the gathering night as if a wrathful sun was turning back on the world. It soon became a fierce beacon.

'Jimmy immediately told the engineer to pile on the coal, speed was what he needed. He knew perfectly well that this would be no salvage job; this offered no prospect of heroically entering port with a rich plum dangling at the end of a towing hawser. This would be an errand of mercy; all he could hope for was to pick up a few survivors, if any of them had been able to get away in time. So, "Speed, more speed, drive her at the very limit!" were his orders.

'The engineers did their utmost, they linked out the cylinder valves, the stokers kept at it and safety valves were lifting most of the time. The bed plates shook and rattled enough to shake the teeth out of one's head, and her speed crept up, from the usual ten knots to eleven, eleven and a half, twelve and a little over. Yet to Jimmy and those on the bridge, she was crawling along.

'The glare grew in size as we hurried across the intervening distance. A broad pillar of heavy dense smoke curling upwards surmounted the fire. It looked as if a monstrous furnace had emptied its load of molten metal on the sea. The pillar carried within its belching blackness, pockets of gas, which ignited at various altitudes giving the awesome impression of the very heavens being invaded by the dreaded tragedy. Then as we got closer, we saw the flames, vivid, bright, yellow and red that leaped around and on the burning ship.

'Jimmy went straight for the fire till he was a bare cable's length off. Then he slowed down, swung to starboard and steamed slowly parallel, keeping 400 to 500 feet of open water between the fire and our ship.

'The heat grew oppressive and I told myself that any human being on that ship must have perished already. In fact I was amazed that the ship was still afloat. My mind reeled at the impact of the intense heat, and could not understand how she had not melted or disintegrated before now. Spillage of oil across the surface of the sea meant the ship was not only burning but was surrounded by burning oil.

'The lightest zephyr of a breeze was coming out of Africa but by the time it reached the scene of disaster it had practically petered out. Yet it was sufficient to impede the spread of the fire across the surface of the sea on the starboard side of the vessel. And, although the expanse of burning oil was a little smaller here, it had packed the flames together into a solid mass of roaring destruction against the ships-side. On the port side, the spread of fire was wider but with several open lanes clear of flames leading towards the ship, some of these lanes were quite wide, others narrow, and on the point of closing. How far these lanes went we could not of course tell, but we watched them eagerly as they were the only means of escape for the crew.

'Jimmy especially studied them intently, got his binoculars on them and scanned them from time to time. There was an appraising look on his strong young face. His only expression was, "My God, what a mess." These were the only words spoken for a long time. He had given instructions to all officers and men to keep a sharp lookout for possible survivors. We circled the fire, which lighted the flat sea for miles around, but there was nothing to be seen outside that circle of hell.

'*Warrior* stopped when she got back to the western side of the fire. Jimmy then said, to no one in particular, although he no doubt meant it for his three officers who were all there on the bridge, as was I, "I am calling for six volunteers to come with me in the small gig. My intention is to try to penetrate as near to *Odin* as possible, to take off or pick up possible survivors." He paused, then added, "I know everyone of you would go if I asked you to, but I consider it right that I shall go, as I am the only unattached officer aboard this ship, except you, Jones (the second mate), but I happen to know you have a girl waiting for you." Then he ordered the second and third to get the boat ready and send word around for six volunteers, but none with wives or families depending on them. "Put a dozen large buckets of fresh water in the gig, also large towels, spare oars, rowlocks. Remove the sails and mast. Be as quick as you can, Mr Morton," he turned to his mate. "You will of course take charge of the ship during my absence. Keep her steady as she is; don't get nearer to the fire."

'He turned and gazed at the fearful scene in front of him, watching the flames and gauging the openings between them. He was deathly calm, austere in a detached way. It was obvious he had rid his mind of any thoughts of risk or danger. He was weighing up the situation, sorting out the difficulties of the job to find the best way of tackling it. He is a seasoned seaman and as such used to weighing up probabilities. He was not going to rush ahead into a sea of flames without first judging the pros and cons, ways and means, but this was different, and a gamble with men's lives because nothing could live within that circle of hungry flames.'

Lefevre continued, 'I could not see why he should risk his own and six other good men on a foredoomed venture at such desperate odds. I am old enough to be his father. I am, like him, a master mariner and have been in many a tight corner at sea and in strange lands, and I am his friend. Surely that should entitle me to speak to him. I thought to dissuade him from this foolhardy attempt, however brave it might be, but looking at him and the calm way he organised the rescue, and considering the plight of the men on *Odin*, their desperate position, thought perhaps there is a chance of some of them getting away and Jimmy's would be their only chance.

'So I said nothing, but when he went into his cabin to change, he said to me with a smile, "I cannot turn my back on these poor devils in there. If I steamed away without making an effort I would never be able to live with myself." I gave him my hand and we shook. I knew then that if it was possible to take a boat in there and bring it back, Jimmy would do it.

'The second officer returned and reported the boat was ready. "And I find, Sir," he said with a grin, "we have nothing but bachelors and widowers on board. I have picked six men, who I think will do."

'Jimmy had changed into a pair of overalls. He left the bridge deck for the after-well-deck from where a pilot ladder was swinging over the ship's side. I remember two of them were still on deck, one wearing a pair of sunglasses. "Let me have those glasses, Watson," he said. They were handed to him. "These are celluloid frames. You hang onto them till we return," and he gave them to me. "Sorry, Watson, the glare will be bad, but we cannot risk your optics catching fire. Over you go." He followed down the ladder with a bright "Cheerio" to the deck.

'I went back to the bridge from where I watched the boat's progress across the clear water. It was a sombre picture, this boatload of sweating labouring men clad in nondescript oddments, some in overalls, some in a queer collection of worn-out jackets and paint splashed trousers.

'They rowed for the largest opening, a lane several boat lengths wide. Jimmy was standing up in the stern, no doubt in an effort to con the boat to gauge the length of the lane and its behaviour. Then they disappeared behind a wall of fire.

'The world stood still. Not a breath of air stirred the heat that lay like a cloying vapour over the sea and ship. Not a ripple marred the shining surface of the sea. Only the appalling expanse of roaring flames, with its widening column of curling smoke and fire, roaring and tumbling forever upwards. The sea and star-specked sky were the stage setting for a gigantic Viking's funeral, the terror of which made the world hold its breath.

'How long I stood there staring at the spot where the boat disappeared I do not know, but suddenly I realised that the lane into which she had gone no longer existed. The flames had met; the outlet was closed.

'My eyes burned; the glare blinded me. I put on Watson's sunglasses to ease the strain and took them off again to see better. I was bathed in perspiration but I could not avert my aching eyes from the burning horror, even for a short second, to give them the rest they were weeping for.

'Believe me, cher Edmond, I prayed to God then as I have never prayed before. I implored the Almighty to allow these seven valiant men to return, not to let them be sacrificed on the altar of compassionate bravery.

'I am not a church man, as you know, but in that hour of fate, when the Universe seemed to be in suspense watching the terrible drama unfolding itself, I turned to Him to intercede for these men who had shown their greatness by daring to put their puny selves against the most formidable of nature's elements.

'And I was not the only one to seek God's mercy, as I presently heard Mr Morton's earnest whisper. "My God, please send them back, guide them, make the flames part so that they may get through."

'Many of those who had never been face to face with death will say that Jimmy and his men returned because they made a good job of it and that their time was not yet, but there was more to it than that. I prefer to think that our prayers helped, that God in Heaven watched over them and guided them back; without His blessing they would never have been able to accomplish the task they had set themselves. Our prayers had been heard and were answered for, shortly after, Mr Morton gasped, "Here they are. My God here they come. Look to the left of where they went in," Now I could see the gig. Mr Morton called out, "There they come, Mr Burton. Boat away."

'"Aye, aye Sir," came an answering call from the sea, and I discovered that one of the life boats had been ready and pulled a short distance across the clear water, in readiness for the returning gig.

'"Can you see them Mr Burton?"

'"Yes Sir, I see them all right."

'"Then pull like the Devil, men," and the boat shot forward as the men put their weight into it.

'A very wise and thoughtful measure as the men in the gig were obviously tired out. Through the binoculars I saw the painstakingly slow stroke, the clumsy, fumbling of oars that had become too heavy for their tired minds and muscles. Jimmy was sitting in the stern sheets; now and again he dipped the bailer overboard to sluice water over the gunnels of this craft that must be smouldering in places. I could see she was lower in the water.

'Their heads were swathed in towels; I counted them; yes, they were all there, swinging their bodies stiffly backwards, forwards, backwards, forwards, mechanically. Gone was the elastic rhythm of the start; they were played out now, only their subconscious minds telling them they must keep on pulling. Then they stopped, not suddenly, smart as if on command; they stopped piecemeal, ruggedly as one after another slumped on the thwarts. Jimmy must have seen the boat coming and told them to stop, an order that took some time to penetrate their tired minds.

'Then I realised they were not alone in the boat. I could dimly discern other figures huddled in the lee of the gunnels, only the distance and the glow made it difficult to see how many.

'They were now reasonably clear of the fire but the heat must have been terrific. Mr Burton's boat reached them; he hooked on a painter and towed the gig back to the ship. The gangway had been lowered and when they came alongside, Jimmy stiffly rose. But I doubt he would have made it if the third officer hadn't been there to help him.

'They did not return empty handed. They had four survivors; one in the bows, two huddled on the floorboards and one laid out at Jimmy's feet. They were in a bad way, and the smell of burnt flesh reached me. The gig's crew also had suffered, either from burns or from blindness, or both; most of them were unable to make the gangway. So, with the survivors and three of the crew, the gig was connected to the hoist and lifted up onto the deck.

'With an effort, Jimmy staggered up the bridge ladder, went to the starboard wing facing the fire; it was now a solid mass of flames, which had spread over an ever widening expanse of the water. There he stood gripping the teak rail till the knuckles showed blue-white against the grime of his hands. He was no longer a young man; Father Time had touched him and drained the years of youth from his body. He was gaunt, his face drawn, ashen, and a vivid red weal running down the left cheek and chin only enhanced the dead colour. Tears were rolling down a face from which eyebrows and most of his moustache had been singed. He was wet, his boots squelched, his overalls were dirty, grime streaked, badly burned in places and stuck to his body like tights.

'He stood there and stared in front of him, immobile. Then, as if he felt he could again master his voice, he said, still staring across to the sea of flames, "Send Sparks to me, Mr Morton. We will get underway as soon as you can get the boats in. My compliments to the chief, and tell him we want all the speed we can get out of her. Then go down and help with the sick. Lay them out on the No. 3 hatch under the awning. Rig the cluster so you can see what you are doing. And send Mr Jones up."

'Sparks who was hovering near now came up, Jimmy dictated cables to his agents in Funchal, Madeira and to his owners. He did it all mechanically; standing there gripping the rail, he was obviously holding himself in check. He had played his game of high endeavour and won; now the reaction was setting in, which required all his willpower to subdue. He was plainly in great pain; how much so I was soon to realise.

'Mr Morton came back with the third officer, the engine room telegraph tingled and the ship came to life again.

'As if the stamp of the engine brought him an awareness of his surroundings and our presence, he began to speak, haltingly.

'"One ... poor ... devil ... out of an alleyway. I called out ... we couldn't get any nearer ... I shouted ... him to dive ... His hand ... came across ... hot deckplates ... like cat ... hot bricks ... got to ... top rail ... supporting himself holding ... stanchion. He was ready ... dive ... but hesitated ... suppose ... flaming sea ... below ... unnerved him. I called ... again ... shouted ... we could not ... wait longer ... flames closing in ... he seemed paralysed ... frozen in that Hades ... then a tongue of flame ... shot out ... alleyway ... licked his legs ... came back ... bigger ... I shouted ... he cried out ... still clung to stanchion ... trousers burning ... all smoke ... then all ... sudden flames burned ... him ... like torch ... when flames drove ... us away ... only charred cross ... one limb ... still sticking ... stanchion ... a man ... cremated alive ... before our eyes ... helpless."

'He was grim, telling this story. Now and again he thumped the teak with his open hand as he choked, swallowed and stumbled over his words. "If he jumped ... could have ... saved ... him."

'The steamer had gathered speed; we were drawing away from the fire when the end came. There was a tremendous upheaval under the black pall of smoke, the burning vessel leaped out of the water like a monstrous glittering gold fish with scales of yellow, red and orange flames. Then she broke in two as the scales flew skywards and burning oil poured out like golden water cascading from a gigantic fountain. The roar of the explosion reached us as the two halves sank back into the hell from which they had sprung to disappear from sight.

'"My God, what an end," Jimmy gulped as he stared spellbound across the heaving desolation where the swell marked the plunge of the once gallant ship and the merciless finish to two score or so of good men.

'Fortunately the good weather held and we arrived at Funchal next morning. The engineer and stokers sweated in the engine room to such good purpose that they pushed her well beyond her expected speed. The No. 3 hatch had been turned into a hospital ' and it was here that misery loomed large and at times seemed to nullify all our efforts. We all turned doctors and nurses, all except Jones, who kept a lone watch on the bridge most of the night. We swabbed, cut away burned flesh, washed, painted with Caron oil, and dressed with Vaseline gauze. We didn't have much to work with and not much knowledge either, but we did our best. Morphia had to be used as some were suffering to such an extent that it was impossible to touch them without first deadening their sensitivities.

'After we left the fire, I got Jimmy down to the hospital. I had to cut away his overalls as well as his underwear. He was burned in places. His clothes stuck to the wounds and suppurating blisters. He was badly burned, especially round the neck and down his back, his hands and wrists. He must have been in terrible pain but as soon as he had been seen to, he was up and assisting in the doctoring of the other sufferers.

'One of the Norwegians died shortly after arriving on board. He was terribly injured; large parts of his body were affected; his head, neck and face were burnt out of recognition. Jimmy said he was their first survivor; they had found him in the water after entering the burning oil. The other three were also in a bad way, but it was hoped that if they could be got to hospital quickly they might survive. All of Jimmy's crew had suffered, three rather badly and were plainly hospital cases.

'That was four years ago. Jimmy is an impressionable young man and the experience of having to face the responsibility and danger suddenly forced upon him must have left scars on his memory.'

Lefevre's story came to an end. Brasserie Moderne was in full swing with diners and winers who were making the evening gay under the bright lights. The two hopefuls at the adjoining table had departed or found better prospects. The gaiety around us was a curious background to the sombre story I had just listened to. We both fell quiet. I thanked him for telling me as we parted.

CHAPTER 11

CAPTAIN BONNET

Belle Île
Catch me if you can!

Of great interest and excitement to all shipping people at Nantes was the story of how the iron barque *Belle Île* and Captain Bonnet outwitted the German submarine.

The *Belle Île* was inward bound with a full cargo of phosphate from Iquique (Chile). She was approaching Cape Finistère for the Bay of Biscay when she spotted a German submarine four to five miles off, showing a flag hoist ordering her to heave to.

Although the odds of a sailing vessel escaping from a submarine were the slenderest, Captain Bonnet decided to make a run for it. There was a topping breeze, the barque was doing twelve to fourteen knots under all sails and she carried a full crew of experienced seaman.

When the German realised she was not stopping, he fired two shots at her, but fortunately both fell short; then he took up the chase.

Belle Île won the first round in eluding the submarine by luffing until she was close hauled on port tack, trimming the yards to sail as fast and close to the wind as these fine craft were able to. Having achieved the object of reducing the potential target area, *Belle Île* gradually bore away till she had the wind over her quarter, her best point of sailing, and the sub was unable to gain on her. The chase continued during the afternoon across a sea that was empty except for the two antagonists.

The master and his men worked with a will, never were wind and sails watched more eagerly, never were halyards and sheets tended with such care, and the two men on the wheel were the best helmsmen in the ship. They possessed the gift of feel, that immediate sense of the slightest shift of wind, and know instinctively, that she will need a little more helm, either port or starboard. And as the spokes of the helm steadily turned, the weight of the ship is gauged to every inch, until they know she has got what she wants.

When the night fell, the killer was still in her wake, perhaps a little nearer. No doubt he hoped for a lessening of the breeze towards sunset and an easy victim at dusk. But the gods smiled on the brave. The wind held and the barque flew into the night.

The captain told his crew what was expected of them, and at ten o'clock the barque tacked. At a sign from the captain standing at the break of the poop, the helm was put down and sheets let go. *Belle Île* carried nearly 4000 tons of phosphate, so she was no light toy and with all sails set was a handful in a strong breeze. But there was none of that commotion usually present when a larger sailing vessel goes about. She swung over sedately, deliberately, a little faster than usual maybe, but without in the least appearing hurried or flustered, preserving even in her hour of danger that dignity which is part of a noble ship.

Except for the creaking of a few blocks and the muffled roll of a few barrels there was no sound. Bells were no longer struck, and of course she carried no lights. She had become a ghost ship swinging around out there, slipping away from her relentless pursuer.

They repeated the performance at 1 am and again at 3 am, hoping to have fooled the sub. They had sailed her round in circles as Lefevre later put it. When the grey dawn showed up the watery waste of billows rolling in from the western ocean, the submarine was nowhere to be seen and *Belle Île* was put on her course for the Loire. She arrived off the pilot station in the early afternoon where she anchored for a tug. She was towed up the river that night and tied up alongside her owner's wharf in Nantes in the early morning.

That was two days ago, and this epic of the sea has been talked about ever since. The local papers carried the story on their front pages with photographs and interviews. The Quai de la Fosse resounded with the praises of the gallant Captain Bonnet and his men.

This of course called for a very large lunch. Lefevre, Captain Bonnet, Captain Bullock and of course myself were all present. Lefevre of course knew Captain Bonnet, had already seen his log and heard the tale in detail from several of the actual participants; more interesting still, he had been allowed to copy *Belle Île's* track chart showing the course sailed from the time she was sighted by the sub and the various tacks during the night until she arrived at the pilot station. He had the chart with him now.

They spread the chart on the table and we all gloated over this excellent piece of seamanship that had robbed the enemy of a valuable prize. It was one of those small victories that occurred from time to time, which alone was not going to win the war but taken together was bound to have an effect.

CHAPTER 12

The U-boat

Of all the weapons designed to fight the war none was more effective or had a greater impact than the German submarine or U-boat.

At the outbreak of World War I Germany had twenty operational submarines (the British Royal Navy had over seventy) but the German submarines were superior vessels with more efficient diesel engines, optically superior periscopes, more powerful wireless transmitters and a cruising range of 5000 miles, giving them a capability of operating in waters around the entire coast of Great Britain.

For centuries, warships had been expected to operate by a set of rules called the 'prize regulations'. These regulations were formalised during the sixteenth century and were at that time agreed upon by all maritime nations.

According to these regulations, a warship during war could stop an unarmed merchant ship; if the ship proved to be neutral it should be let go, but if it belonged to the enemy both ship and cargo could be taken as a prize and the passengers and crew as hostages. If no prize crew could be provided to seize the ship intact, then the ship could be sunk but only after the crew and passengers had been removed.

Plainly, submarines were ill suited to abide by these prize regulations; a submarine could not stop and search a ship without exposing itself and certainly could not spare men for a prize crew. But prior to World War I most naval strategists thought the submarines would only be used against enemy warships (von Terpitz and Winston Churchill) and very few visualised submarines being used indiscriminately against unarmed merchant ships. They were in for a very rude shock. Submarine warfare as pursued by Germany was to escalate in a step-like fashion culminating in unrestricted submarine warfare, meaning the indiscriminate sinking of all ships approaching the British Isles.

The most successful of the German U-boats (Unterseeboote) ranged in size from 516 to 800 tons. They had six torpedo tubes, one or two 10.5 or 15 cm deck guns and carried a crew of between thirty and forty men. Their maximum underwater speed was six to eight knots, their surface speed twelve to sixteen knots. Such was the weapon that was to be the most potent to be used in World War I.

The first action against merchant shipping occurred on 20 October 1914 when, off the Norwegian coast, U17 surfaced and did stop a British cargo ship and did allow the crew to take to the lifeboats before sinking the ship. This initial practice of playing by the rules did not last long, for a number of very good reasons, one of which was Britain's blockade of western Europe.

British warships blockading Germany were able to stop all ships proceeding to Europe, including neutral Scandinavia and Holland, search the ships, seize any contraband and then allow some neutral ships to proceed. This practice put the Germans at a considerable disadvantage, as all worthwhile goods were seized by the British without any loss of life.

To counter this policy, German submarine warfare took a step up and all belligerent ships (i.e. British, French, Russian and Belgian) were to be sunk without warning (but at that time not neutral ships). As a result, many passengers travelling on British and French ships died, irrespective of their nationality. This escalation culminated in the sinking without warning of the prestigious British Cunard liner *Lusitania* on 5 May 1915 with the loss of 1198 lives (including ninety-four children) and consequent worldwide condemnation of Germany, particularly in America.

The *Lusitania*

RMS Lusitania, 31,550 tons. Once holder of the blue ribbon for the fastest east–west crossing of the Atlantic, she was sunk by U20 on 7 May 1915.

On Friday, 7 May 1915, Lieutenant Walter Schwieger was sitting jacketless in the conning tower of U20, chewing a sandwich and listening to the sub's gramophone. Having already sunk three ships on this patrol, he was heading for home, low on fuel but still carrying three torpedos. Shortly after 1 pm he noticed a smudge of smoke off his starboard bow. U20 dived and the smudge of smoke now viewed through the periscope quickly grew into a large four funnelled liner. Schwieger attacked and sank the *Lusitania*.

Of all the horrors of the sea war, none had a greater emotional impact than the sinking of the Cunard liner *Lusitania*.

The *Lusitania* was launched on 7 June 1906. She displaced 31,550 tons and on her first run across the Atlantic captured the Blue Ribbon for the fastest westward Atlantic crossing; and in spite of the war, trans-Atlantic crossings continued, usually with a full compliment of passengers.

At the outbreak of war, she was looked over by the British admiralty for possible use as an armed merchant cruiser but was found to burn too much coal for war duties. Indeed, because of her high demand for coal, 'boiler room four' was closed, reducing her speed to twenty-one knots, still ten knots faster than any U-boat. However, the *Lusitania* was required to reserve cargo space for the express purpose of carrying American war materials to Britain; this she did on each voyage.

When the *Lusitania* embarked from America for England on 1 May 1915, the cargo included nearly 300 tons of ammunition, and, despite printed warnings from the German Embassy in America, only one passenger changed his travel plans. The *Lusitania* sank in eighteen minutes, and 1198 men, women and children perished, including 124 American neutrals.

The sinking of the *Lusitania* was a propaganda bonanza for the allies and did much to change American opinion. The Germans were portrayed as barbaric killers with no regard for innocent civilians. The fact that the *Lusitania* was carrying munitions was suppressed.

As if the sinking of the *Lusitania* did not do enough damage to German prestige world wide, they, the Germans, went on to commit a crime that was also a colossal propaganda blunder. At dawn on 11 October, they executed by firing squad a civilian British nursing sister, Edith Cavell, who had been working in Belgium since 1910.

Nurse Cavell was found guilty of assisting British servicemen stranded behind enemy lines to escape into neutral Holland. It is true that she was not the first woman to be judicially killed during World War I. The French had previously shot Marguerite Schmitt for spying for Germany.

Nurse Cavell's execution evoked special horror, for she was not a paid British agent but a civilian nursing sister who was simply trying voluntarily to help fellow citizens to escape. Marguerite Schmitt was a trained and paid German spy.

The next step up in Germany's U-boat campaign occurred as a result of Germany's problems with a war on two fronts.

During 1916, the war had reached a stalemate. Neither side could breach the front line in Northern France; while at sea, the battle of Jutland (13 May 1916) between the British and German fleets had proved inconclusive. Stalemate in the west meant that Germany continued to face Russia.

To try and resolve this situation, Germany made a fatal mistake that was to cost her the war. She had overestimated the strength of Russia (in contradiction to her assessment during World War II) and underestimated the strength and resolve of Great Britain. Based on this assessment, Germany decided to try to force a negotiated peace in the west, which would then allow her to concentrate on one front, against Russia.

The Telegram

At the beginning of the nineteenth century, Mexico included what is now California, Nevada, Texas, Arizona, Colorado and New Mexico. By 1848, all these territories had been forcibly taken from her and incorporated into the United States. It was indeed a huge area of land.

On the 17 January 1917, a wireless message from the German Foreign Secretary to the German Ambassador in Washington was intercepted by British intelligence. It read:

We intend to begin unrestricted submarine warfare. We shall endeavour to keep the US neutral. In the event of this not succeeding we will make Mexico a proposal of alliance so she might recover her lost lands.

This information was immediately transmitted by British Intelligence to the United States Government.

On the 31 January 1917, Berlin formally notified Washington that unrestricted warfare would begin next day, 1 February 1917. On 3 February, the USA broke off relationships with Germany and declared war on her on 2 April 1917.

To achieve this result, Germany decided to place her trust in her submarines. Henceforth, all ships approaching the British Isles were to be sunk on sight irrespective of their nationality. This was unrestricted submarine warfare. As a result, British shipping losses rose dramatically and reached a peak in April 1917 when 155 of her ships, totalling 519,394 tons, went to the bottom. The intensity of this campaign nearly brought Britain to her knees, but not quite.

On 2 April 1917, the United States declared war on Germany. This move was certainly precipitated to a great extent by Germany's decision to introduce unrestricted submarine warfare and long before any suggestion that Britain would seek a negotiated peace. Then, in June 1917, the dissolution of Russian military power became apparent without the help of submarines and by October 1917 Russia was seeking peace with Germany.

It now became clear to Germany that her war on two fronts was nearly over, but not in the way hoped for. It was an irreparable tragedy for Germany that she had commenced unrestricted submarine warfare only a few months before the stalemate it was designed to break dissolved without it. Germany now had a one front war (albeit the wrong front) but had now to face fresh troops, the industrial might of America and, unexpectedly, the necessity to still deploy nearly a million troops in eastern Europe to maintain law and order and make them therefore unavailable to be relocated to the western front.

Reference: David Shermer, *World War I* (London, Peter Dunbar Associations, 1973). Correlli Barnett, *The Sword Bearers* (London, Hodder & Stoughton, 1986).

The Convoy

During April 1917 German submarines sent to the bottom 837,000 tons of shipping, this included neutral ships. This prompted the first Sea Lord, Sir John Jellico to predict swift defeat at sea if this rate of sinking continued. Obviously a change of thinking was urgently needed. In short a convoy system.

Convoys were not new. England utilised them in the Napoleonic wars and even to a limited extent during World War I. Small convoys were utilised across the channel to France and across the North Sea to Sweden and Norway. However, the admiralty had been reluctant to inaugurate a convoy system across the Atlantic for two reasons: a perceived shortage of escorts and the fear that ships in convoy would not keep station because of variation in their size and power and particularly in rough weather at night.

Part of the admiralty's problem was its misinterpretation of statistics, including the incredible howler of accepting, for planning purposes, the figure for total weekly departures from British ports as 5000 vessels, when this figure included coastal shipping and cross channel ferries not requiring escorts. In truth, there were adequate escorts, particularly following America's entry into the war.

The first long haul convoy, of seventeen ships, sailed from Gibraltar in May 1917 and another, of twelve ships, from America; both arrived without loss. Here indeed lay the answer in spite of all the misgivings. By August 1917, all British bound ships with a speed of less than twelve knots (equalling the surface speed of German U-Boats) were convoyed and by October 1917 more than 1500 ships had been convoyed into British ports with the loss of only ten ships.

During four years of war, German U-boats accounted for 6394 merchant ships and 107 war ships:

Date	Ships	Tons
1914	3	2950
1915	640	1,189,031
1916	1301	2,194,420
1917	3170	5,938,023
1918	1280	2,624,278

In addition, U-boats sank ten battleships, seventeen cruisers and eighty other warships.

Reference: Antony Preston, *Submarines* (Boston, Boston Books, 1982).

CHAPTER 13

TERESE

I have never seen Terese but I am told that she was provincial French and pretty. Perhaps she looked something like this in 1915. The author.

Gladiator was diverted to St Nazaire for several voyages, so I did not see Captain Bullock for some time. He would occasionally phone through if he had any special problem or if the charterers had any queries. But the vessel maintained her regular run in the coal trade; the charterers were happy with her and her personnel. We had every reason to expect that things would continue, barring accidents, after all the war was still on.

Captain Lefevre, who was in charge of the Loire Pilot Service, went down to St Nazaire frequently and met Bullock now and again when he was in port. He told me Jimmy had become very friendly with Terese, one of the girls who occasionally joined the clientèle at Café des Arts. Evidently Terese commuted between Nantes and St Nazaire when the *Gladiator* was expected in. 'Oh yes, Jimmy is comfortably fixed in St Nazaire,' he assured me. How comfortably, I was soon to learn.

Terese met me on the way to the office one day with, 'Good morning, Monsieur Edmond, may I speak with you?' Sensing that this was more than an ordinary morning greeting I led her into a nearby bistro and offered her a cassis. She very quickly came to the point, and it was all about Captain Bullock. How she had first met him in Nantes and now in St Nazaire. She goes there to meet him as soon as she gets the cable from Cardiff that he is on his return voyage. 'He is a great friend, a wonderful man and he wants me to be with him all the time. He wants me to marry him. To go with him to England to be Mrs Bullock. He is the nicest man I have ever met; he is what you call a gentleman. Yes, I love him, and I am sure he loves me too. I could be very happy with him; it would be marvellous. But it is a serious matter this getting married and going to a strange land – a strange language. I am twenty-three years of age; you know Jimmy very well and you know me and my background a little. I am sure I will make a good wife for the right man, and I know Jimmy is the right man; only sometimes I get a bit frightened. Suppose he one day in a fit of temper throws it up to me that he picked me up at Café des Arts. That would be too brutal. I could not stand it.'

I assured her Jimmy would never be brutal, Jimmy is the most considerate of persons and would never behave like that

– and more in the same vein. I don't know if I sounded very convincing; in fact, I am not sure that I wanted to be convincing. All this was rather more than I had expected, and I realised I was not cast in the mould of marriage counsellor. It was very obvious that she had become greatly attached to Jimmy, and very little was needed for her to take the final step. Jimmy was evidently just as attracted to her as she to him; it was evident that this was no ordinary fly-by-night cheap entanglement. I told myself that, after all, Jimmy's love affairs were his to sort out, and not for me to get concerned about. But I must say that during the months I had known Jimmy, he had so to speak grown on me and I looked upon him as a friend. Lefevre's description of the *Odin's* rescue attempt had of course enhanced his status in my eyes considerably, a man who could not be lightly ignored. I felt I could not stand aside and see him commit himself to an act that might lead him to lifelong unhappiness, a misfit marriage. I wanted to discuss the problem with someone and Lefevre was obviously the man.

Lefevre had known about the affair for some time. He had seen Terese on the St Nazaire train; he had also seen them together. His first reaction was, 'It is none of our business, you know, if Jimmy prefers Terese, why not. He is not married so far as I know, and she is an attractive young woman.' But when I mentioned Terese's words that he wanted to marry her, he refused to believe it. 'There is nothing in it,' he assured me. 'She is just filling a place for another woman. When his charter is finished and he goes on a different run, he will soon forget her and find someone else, and so will she.' I reminded him of his own words that Jimmy is impressionable and not a little emotional, but no, he would not take any talk of marriage seriously. 'I have seen too many of these attachments, they all fizzle out after a while.' Lefevre was to be proved wrong.

About a month later, Jimmy with Terese walked into the office. They had come up by train from St Nazaire where the *Gladiator* was discharging her usual coal cargo. I could feel there was a special reason for this visit, and Terese with a proud gesture extends her hand to show me her ring.

'Terese and I were married in Cardiff last trip,' Jimmy said proudly. Well, well, congratulations all round, in which the rather austere Goupil as well as the staff and Raymond all joined in. 'We would like you to have dinner with us tonight; we are staying at the Louvre Hotel, going back to the ship later,' said Jimmy. He then told me he had planned the thing very carefully. She had gone to Cardiff with him on the last trip. On the previous voyage he had arranged with a minister to marry them in church. The chief officer and engineer were witnesses and his sister had come down from Newcastle for the occasion.

It was a quiet wedding of course, typical of wartime conditions, but his sister had played her part and got on well with Terese. So when the *Gladiator* completed her loading at Cardiff, they left the hotel where they were staying and sailed back to St Nazaire, husband and wife.

And in a quiet way we celebrated their home coming that night at the Louvre. Lefevre had the surprise of his life when he was rounded up, but was soon in fine form, complete with Mrs Lefevre. He more or less took charge of the ceremonies, made the speech for the newlyweds with all his Gallic flourish, and kissed the bride twice. I was surprised to find Terese's mother there. I suppose I never thought in terms of Terese having relations, a father or mother. But Terese had brought her in from one of the estates where she was working, a typical country hand, bright and cheerful. There was obviously great affection between the two. The mother was pleased to see her daughter married well, although she did not like her going away, especially in these troublesome times. Terese looked radiant and happy, as the newspapers would say, quietly dressed with a sprig of forget-me-nots on her lapel. Jimmy was of course proud of her as well as of himself.

There had not been much time, but we all managed to produce a souvenir as a wedding gift for the occasion, and the hotel staff made a fine feature of an attractive table with beautiful floral decorations.

During the evening Jimmy told me he intended to take a short holiday in England, leaving the *Gladiator* to Mr Tyrer, the mate, for a couple of voyages. 'I don't know if it will be much of a holiday with all the restrictions on in England, but it will give Terese a break, initiate her into the family and our way of life. We will be going back to the ship the day after tomorrow when the cargo will be out of her; then we sail for Cardiff and home. After that, we will see what conditions at sea are like.'

I told him I would be leaving France soon, for good, as I had been appointed to a position in Hong Kong. On mentioning the name of the firm I was joining, he told me they are the agents for his family concern, and that they have had two ships trading there for several years, one more or less permanently between South China and Siam, Federated Malay States and Singapore, and another on charter in the same region including Java.

We met again the following evening for apéritifs and dinner at Lefevre's. They live in the old family home, an ancient stone and brick house like several similar ones in Nantes, lending dignity to a tree-lined boulevard not far from the river. It was probably built in the era of the Edict of Nantes – 1598. It contained a huge kitchen with a formidable stove between two windows and a wonderful collection of highly polished pots and pans. The floor was brick-lined and in keeping with the elderly maid who obviously ruled the ménage in her clogs. I would guess she probably saw Mrs Lefevre into this world and had been watching over her family ever since. A true Bretonne, or shall we say, Nantaise. There was also a younger servant in support.

Madame produced a tremendous dinner, Lefevre the wines, and it became a truly festive occasion. Their two sons were on leave, both in uniforms, the elder from the army and the younger from the navy. They were both full of fun and the perfect foil for their exuberant father.

Captain Bonnet of the *Belle Île* was there with his wife; he was having a spell ashore for a while. Moser my colleague in the office was there with his latest and two or three others whose names I have forgotten. It was truly a memorable dinner. Jimmy said to me as we parted, 'So we shan't be losing touch.' Very prophetic words as it happened, as there was to be a long gap before I was to see any of them again.

*   *   *

For continuity I must jump two years. It was in Hong Kong in 1917 that I received the sad news that the *Gladiator* had been torpedoed and sunk in the Irish Sea. The news was brief as usual in those days, but I was glad to hear that all the crew had been saved. It was fortunate that, at the time, we had another of the company's ships in port, SS *Warrior*; so I got in touch with her captain, Captain Swanson, hoping he might have some details; but unfortunately he had nothing to add.

Then, unexpectedly, Captain Tyrer turned up having come out on a naval oiler. He had been with his old ship (as first mate) when she went down. It was the usual story: a German sub appeared to starboard and sent two torpedoes into her – one into her side bunkers and the other aft that smashed the machinery and steering gear.

'She settled down quite gently,' said Tyrer. 'We had everything ready, our lifeboats had been permanently swung out in their davits fully provisioned with water and ships biscuits. We were ready for the emergency, thanks to the skipper (Captain Bullock). Fortunately, the weather was fine but very cold. We got two lifeboats away with twenty-four men and Terese. Yes, she was there. Once on the water we kept the two boats together and started rowing towards land which we reckoned to be about a hundred miles away. We were torpedoed about 10 am, but it was only next noon that we were picked up by a naval trawler; and, believe you me, we were mighty glad to leave those lifeboats.'

'How did Terese face up to it?' I asked.

'She was wonderful,' Tyrer said. 'One of the stokers smashed his knee getting into the boat and Terese looked after him. It got very cold that night and I think she rather felt it then, but she was bright and cheery, and a great boost to morale. She had travelled a few voyages with us to Cardiff and back to Nantes and had become quite a favourite with all of us.'

Well, well I thought, she has turned out trumps. That little lady that had been picked up in a Nantes café. 'What now?' I asked.

'Well, Captain Bullock is having a bit of leave, but if the war goes on much longer he will soon get to sea again. I hear the skipper of the *Battler* also wants release and of course there is sure to be another *Gladiator*.' Little did I know our paths were to cross again in the not too distant future.

PART FIVE

Trans-Siberia, 1916

CHAPTER 14

The Journey

The Trans-Siberian Railway was opened for passenger traffic in 1916, just before my father took the journey and only a few months before the first revolution in Russia (February–March 1917).

Sverre Odmûnd Berg at the age of 24.
Photo taken in 1916 prior to his departure from France to Hong Kong.

I have recently received an offer from a well known Norwegian shipping firm, Thoresen & Co., for a position in their Hong Kong office. This was to me an exciting offer and a great step up.

I had certainly enjoyed my time in France and had learnt a great deal, not only about shipping but life in general. It was time to move on.

While in Nantes I had had the opportunity to visit Paris on a number of occasions. Paris, of course, is always wonderful, but during the war it was like visiting another planet. The war, the money, the soldiers, the girls, the shows and everyone determined to play as if it were their last days on earth (sadly for many, it was). In short it was an exciting place.

It was of course quite amazing how well we lived in Nantes; no shortages, plenty of interesting company and, when not working, a very pleasant bistro-type life. But the time had come to pack and say goodbye to friends I had made, in particular Lefevre, M Goupil, the office staff, Madame Rollins, Captain Bonnet, Terese, Jimmy and others.

Understandably, to get out of France during those days was not easy. Travelling was beset with all sorts of restrictions, and being a Norwegian citizen and hence a 'neutral' was an additional problem. (Norway, Sweden, Denmark and Holland were neutral during World War I.)

I called on the Norwegian consul for help and guidance and they proved to be a great help. I was told to report to the Legation in Paris where I was given a small parcel of official papers to deliver to the foreign office in Oslo (named Kristiana until 1925). So I travelled as a semi-official courier.

From there on it became easy. The following evening I left Le Havre in a very tightly packed ship for Southampton. Hundreds of people thronged the wharf hoping to get across to England but with my diplomatic papers I had no problems.

Next morning I was travelling north by train to Newcastle where I hoped to get a Norwegian ship across to Bergen. I was in luck and left for Bergen on the following day. The trip across was rough but fortunately we did not meet any German submarines. On reaching Bergen I spent a day with friends then crossed by train to Oslo where I delivered the diplomatic parcel to the foreign office. Having become wise in the ways of the world I took the opportunity of mentioning that I would shortly be going to Russia and then by the Trans-Siberian Railway to the Far East. As I had hoped, they very kindly offered to provide me with another parcel of diplomatic mail for their Hong Kong office.

While in Oslo I had a meeting with the directors of Thoresen, my new bosses, then took the overnight train to Trondheim to see my parents. Then after a week at home, back to Oslo, picked up the diplomatic parcel and collected a few odds and ends and prepared myself for a very long train trip.

I set off by train from Oslo, travelled through southern Norway, Sweden and Finland and then south through St Petersburg (Petrograd) to Moscow. It was the long way around but in 1916 it was the only way into Russia.

The train was comfortable. I shared a two berth cabin with a young Englishman who was on his way to Moscow to join the British Legation (another Jimmy). In the next cabin was a young American selling artificial limbs (there was a big market for these in 1916!). In fact, he wore a large golden artificial leg from his watch chain.

It was April and the country looked beautiful. We passed through Sweden and miles and miles of pine forests, there were not many stops on this first run so it was a relatively fast trip. Finally we arrived at Haparanda on the Tornio River, the boundary between Sweden and Finland, at the top end of the Gulf of Bothnia.

I certainly was not prepared for what occurred at Haparanda. We had to await the arrival of two very long troop trains full of seriously wounded soldiers for repatriation to their own country. The Finnish train arrived from Russia with German wounded, the Swedish train with Russian wounded. The trains were halted at opposite sides of the river and did not pull up at a common platform.

This meant that wounded men had to be unloaded and transported across the river. It was a horrible sight: badly wounded men, some with amputated limbs, horribly scarred faces, severe burns and abdominal wounds were lifted out of carriages on opposite sides of the river and often left on the open ground for sometime before being carried across the railway bridge or ferried across the partly frozen river to the other train. Some died during the transfer; it was in truth a horrible experience and I was glad when we were allowed to proceed through Finland.

Finland is the land of a thousand lakes and although different to Sweden, there were still green forests and surprisingly quite a deal of sand like dust. We passed through Helsinki and after a short stop, proceeded to Russia. Shortly after crossing the border we arrived at Petrograd (St Petersburg or Leningrad) for a one day stop.

I was very impressed with what I saw in Petrograd with its massive government buildings, imposing palaces and beautiful gardens, but time did not allow a visit to the Hermitage, Art Gallery or Winter Palace.

*   *   *

We arrived in Moscow at day break; it was cold and there were still signs of winter in left over snow piles on street corners. As the three of us had first class bookings, we were transferred to adjoining rooms in a first class hotel.

The immediate need was for hot baths. We rang our bells for service and three rather attractive young housemaids appeared. But language difficulties made further progress nil. None of us could speak Russian, except the girls of course. We tried them with English, French, Italian, Norwegian and the American produced some doubtful Indian, but to no avail. Then one bright spark sprouted some German. That rang a bell and caused some excitement. The German language was taboo of course, and the girls were terrified of being found using the forbidden tongue. They were all willing and very friendly, so we all started talking in whispers like a secret society. The girls spoke fluent German; there was no doubt that it was their mother tongue. So far as we were concerned it worked wonders and we got marvellous attention. They even arranged breakfast for us in one of our rooms. I have often wondered what these obviously attractive German girls were doing in that hotel when their own country was at war with Russia and, a little sadly, what happened to them when the Bolsheviks took over.

The trio who had so far travelled together from Oslo now dispersed. Jimmy went to his Legation and Golden Leg went to the USA Red Cross to negotiate his skill. I went for a solitary drive that afternoon, sightseeing. I saw a couple of kilometres of the outside of the Kremlin but as there were no embalmed heroes in glass coffins to gaze at in those days (Lenin was still alive) I soon got bored.

On returning to the hotel, my attractive whispering maid appeared bringing beer, which was most welcome; it had to be virtually smuggled into my room. She made my short stay in Moscow very enjoyable.

Next morning I boarded my train for the long haul. I was surprised to find the passenger carriages were all 'wagon-lits' cars (sleeping carriages made in Belgium); it appeared that a French company had leased the first class section of the train. It was very comfortable with two sleeping bunks in each compartment together with the usual amenities. Sharing the cabin with me was a Russian major about thirty-five. He had just been transferred from the German front to a new appointment further south. He was a very pleasant fellow and spoke very good English. Unfortunately he didn't stay with us for long and left the following afternoon.

I don't know what travelling by the Trans-Siberian Railway is like today, but when I made the trip I found it interesting and a most friendly train. The train was by no means packed and after the major left, I had the compartment all to myself for most of the trip.

A number of Russian officials came and went, getting on and off at intermediate places. There were a few commercial travellers and a number of army officers. Surprisingly, there were three English businessmen going to Mukden (Manchuria) who never stopped playing bridge. They had to have a fourth of course and they called me in. I have never been a card man and never will be. I have never played bridge, except on Sunday afternoons with the old aunties at the boarding house in Glasgow. I told them I knew nothing about the game, but they were in dire straits so I filled in from time to time. I trumped my partner's ace more than once, but they had to have a fourth so they put up with my atrocious bridge.

Then there was Louise, a young Swedish girl who was going to Yokohama to marry her fiancé who was stationed there. She was travelling with an elderly lady who had taken on the duties of chaperone. Louise was a good violinist, and as I also had my violin with me, we occasionally got together for a couple of 'moments musicals'. Very pleasant but I have a feeling that the watch-hound sitting in the corner did not enjoy it overmuch. She took her duties very, very seriously.

We had a couple of Dutch officials going to Osaka (Japan), I think with a contract for building ships. This rather interested me of course, although I was rather surprised at the timing, as Japan had just entered the war on the allied side and the Dutch, I felt, were a little pro-German?

We also had an American with us. He had come across from Svalbard, (Spitzbergen) by ship to Narvik and then by train into Sweden, through Finland and down to Moscow, as I had. A quiet chap but he did not play bridge, so he was no help to me. 'The only card game I know is Poker,' he assured me and I, like him, was hoping the others would switch to the more 'he-man' game, but the bridge players refused to be tempted. He had some wonderful tales to tell about Svalbard; he had been travelling around in the Arctic for some two seasons taking photographs and was now on his way to Japan to ascend and photograph the sacred mountain, Fujiyama.

We are now fast approaching the Urals, the mountain range

that divides Russia from Asia. The Urals have been described in various ways by many writers and there is a certain grimness to the very name. Whether this is justified or not I am not prepared to say. The country itself appears harsh; there is no lusciousness about it, although forests are seen from time to time. The Urals in those days were known as one of the richest mineral areas of the world and the quantity and variety of different minerals found and mined in the Urals have earned it the sobriquet 'The Museum of Minerals'. The Urals are today one of the richest assets of the USSR.

The industrialisation of the area was already very apparent and we saw ample evidence of this as we rumbled along, stopping at intervals for short spells. I often got off the train and strolled along the platform and, if time permitted, into the nearest streets. Finally we arrived at Yekaterinburg (Ekaterinburg and now Sverdlovsk) the largest city in the area. We had a couple of hours there, had some very good hot food at the railway canteen and a short walk around the nearby area. Factories big and small, mostly big, everywhere, with huge smoke stacks belching forth. It was here at Yekaterinburg that Tsar Nicholas II and his entire family were later murdered by the Bolsheviks following the revolution in 1918. A most grisly and inhuman act for which I believe the Russians will forever be condemned.

Our wagon-lits carriages were shunted off the train at Yekaterinburg, their place taken by Russian cars, which were practically identical and comfortable and the two attendants that have been with us from the start are still doing their jobs. Strictly speaking, Yekaterinburg is where the Trans-Siberian Railway takes over from the Russian European system and starts its long journey to Vladivostok.

We have now been on the road for four days and life has taken on a steady routine that seems to have become a way of life. In the morning I walk along the train and, if it happens to stop at one of the smaller stations, take my container to draw hot water for shaving from the engine driver. He is a friendly hirsute fellow and always greets me with 'Ah, mon General'. The forenoon passes fairly quickly with a bit of reading or writing, in the afternoon a little music or I may try and help out the bridge players. Dinner in the dining car is always the showpiece; we ginger ourselves up a bit and give discussions full play.

Our next significant stop is Omsk, a fairly large Siberian town. The countryside now changes; the land is flat, we pass numerous lakes and forests interspaced with open grasslands and then across the River Ob and onto Tomsk. It is a harsh land where winter temperatures drop to 20° below freezing.

We eventually arrive at Irkutsk on Lake Baikal, the largest and deepest fresh water lake in Asia. Fed by no less than 300 streams, the lake is surrounded by mountains and the landscape becomes much more interesting.

As the train pulled into Irkutsk station we could hear lively music from Balalaikas and other string instruments. Next we see troops of young girls and men performing in the square near the station. Dressed in Cossack costumes they gave a very attractive performance.

To our delight they joined the train and were to remain with us all the way to Vladivostok. The rest of the journey was great fun. In the evening the troop took complete charge of the dining car. After dinner all removable furniture was cleared away, vodka flowed, dancing and music began. The girls were excellent dancing partners and the men wonderful musicians. So there we were dancing on this swaying train rushing through the night with the strains of Balalaikas wafting across the Siberian countryside. It was certainly a time to remember.

We finally came to Khabarovsk on the Amur River, the largest Russian town east of Irkutsk. The train now crosses the mighty Amur River and goes straight south for Vladivostok. This was the last stretch and packing was the order of the day. The country was not particularly inviting, the weather was lousy but I had made some friends whom I would certainly like to meet again, but sadly this was unlikely.

Eventually we rumbled into Vladivostok and I betook myself to the hotel, whilst most of the others continued a bit further to Nakhovda where there was another terminal. I still don't know the difference between the two terminals as they were only a couple of miles apart, but it meant I saw no more of my erstwhile travelling companions.

I booked into a hotel and next morning on coming down to breakfast I found a Norwegian lady partaking of a very healthy breakfast. She had just come in from up country where she had been collecting fossils and other strange prehistoric items for Oslo University. She is a doctor who had lived in Japan and Shanghai for some time and was now on her way to rejoin her husband who is practising medicine in Shanghai. A most interesting personality, about middle aged and as she was going to Shanghai via Nagasaki (Japan) we left together by the afternoon boat for Japan. After another day sightseeing in Nagasaki we boarded another ship for Shanghai.

I arrived in Shanghai on a Red Cross fête day. Shanghai in those days before the communists and the Japanese spoilt it all, was a fabulous place of high living with no brakes. We were promptly caught up in the festivities but I suffered badly on account of the heat until my new friends the good doctors took pity on me and lent me a tropical suit. I got a ship two days later for Hong Kong, and arrived three days later in the afternoon. Hong Kong looked lovely to me; the harbour with its surrounding hills is one of the beauties of the world. I was home, hosed and dried.

CHAPTER 15

The Trans-Siberian Railway

'Let the railway be built' – *Tsar Alexander III 1886*
'If the train stops all is lost' – *Lenin*

The Siberian boundary post, 1880.
Friends and relatives bid prisoners farewell.
(Transiberian Handbook, Thomas Bryn)

The Trans-Siberian Railway was completed in 1916. The longest railway line in the world, no sooner was it completed than it became a vital supply line to European Russia during the world war. It then became of great strategic importance during the Russian civil war. This is the story of those formative years.

The first railway to be built in Russia was for Tsar Nicholas I in 1836. This line ran ten miles from the capital St Petersburg to his summer palace at Tsarskoye Selo (Czarskoye Selo). So impressed was the Tsar that he ordered the laying down of railway lines in European Russia (i.e. west of the Urals) and in 1878 this system was extended from Perm across the Urals to Yekaterinburg (Sverdlovsk).

During the eighteenth and nineteenth centuries, Russia had extended her empire eastward across Siberia to eventually come into conflict with China. In 1860, Russia by agreement with China obtained all territory north of the Amur River (i.e. north of Manchuria) together with the eastern maritime province between the Ussuri River (a tributary of the Amur) and the Sea of Japan; this included Vladivostok, so that Russian territory now extended to the Pacific.

For Russia to benefit from this huge expanse of territory, some means of transport was needed, the obvious answer was a railway. Initially a very rough road known as the 'Post Road' extended across southern Siberia to Vladivostok. So called 'posting stations' were set up at approximately 25-mile intervals (i.e. approximately forty vestas) along this road; these stations consisted of little more than primitive shelters and between these stations the nineteenth century traveller faced wolves, bears, Siberian tigers, escaped convicts and bandits. The western beginning of the 'Post Road', the official entrance into Siberia from European Russia, was marked by a large black pillar or obelisk on the slopes of the Urals.

In 1881 Alexander III became Tsar. He was a big man in more ways than one. Alexander ordered construction of a railway line between St Petersburg and Moscow. It is said that when his engineers put a map on the table for authorisation, Alexander picked up a ruler and drew a straight line between the two cities and said that was to be the track, irrespective of towns or natural objects and that no expense was to be spared. In short, get on with it.

Five years later, Tsar Alexander III gave the construction of the Trans-Siberian Railway his official sanction. This was to be a broad gauge line confined to Russian territory through to Vladivostok on the Pacific Ocean. In agreement with China, he also authorised the construction of a shorter route through Chinese Manchuria in order to have an alternative and shorter route to Vladivostok.

The shorter route was referred to as the Chinese Eastern Railway or Manchurian Railway, which passed through Harbin. Later, a spur line was built to connect Harbin to Port Arthur at the tip of the Laotung Peninsula and referred to as the South Manchurian Railway, which passed through Mukden.

The Trans-Siberian Railway was to be built, unlike the St Petersburg to Moscow line, as cheaply as possible; as a result, sub-standard sleepers and steel rails were used and bridges were to be constructed of timber. Because of the sub-standard equipment and lack of adequate ballast under the line, rails buckled, rides were bumpy and at times the trains' speed was limited to thirteen miles per hour. This necessitated a massive rebuilding program long before the line was completed.

Construction commenced in 1891 at multiple centres. Labour was recruited from throughout Europe; convicts were used, as were Chinese coolies. Working conditions were appalling and equipment primitive. Winters were long and cold and shelters inadequate. The summers were short, accompanied by plagues of black flies and mosquitos. Outbreaks of bubonic plague (1899) and cholera (1902) decimated the work force. Horses died of anthrax; Amur tigers took live stock and Chinese coolies in the eastern section, while bandits were common, necessitating the stationing of soldiers along the construction sites.

Eventually the line was completed in early 1916 at an estimated cost of $US320 million, a vast amount of money at that time.

From Chelyabinsk and Yekaterinburg where the Trans-Siberian Railway connects with the Russian European system, the line passes through Omsk, Tomsk, Krasnoyarsk and Irkutsk, then skirts Lake Baikal and proceeds to Chita. Shortly beyond Chita the line branches. The south eastern line crosses the frontiers into China at Manchuria Station and proceeds thereafter as the Chinese Eastern Railway across Manchuria, through Harbin and thence eastwards to re-enter Russian territory and Vladivostok. The main northern line east of Chita remains in Russian territory, skirts the northern bank of the Amur River to Khababovsk and then runs due south to Vladivostok.

The line from Moscow to Vladivostok is 9288 kilometres (5222 miles) long, spanning eight time zones. But strictly speaking, the true length of the actual Trans-Siberian Railway is 4200 miles from Yekaterinburg to Vladivostok.

In 1914 Russia went to war with the German and Austrian empires and it soon became apparent that Russian industries were inadequate to support a 'modern war' effort involving an army of well over five million men. This meant that a great deal of equipment and supplies had to be obtained from overseas (e.g. America) and trans-shipped to Russia's western front via the Trans-Siberian Railway. Unfortunately, by late 1916, the railway had almost ceased to function due to heavy traffic of war materials, poor management and antiquated rolling stock. This was in spite of the fact that the line had only recently been laid. As a result, military supplies purchased from the United States and shipped across the Pacific were piling up at Vladivostok.

Following the first revolution in February–March 1917, the provisional government under Alexander Kerensky decided, against strong opposition, to continue the war against Germany and requested help from America to upgrade the line.

Following a survey of the line, the US government called for volunteer American railway men to serve in Russia, not as military personnel but as railway advisors. So came into being the Russian Railway Service Corporation (RRSC). This corps was authorised to consist of 339 officers but only about two-thirds of this number made it through the selection process and were sent to the Russian far east. Fortunately, following the second revolution (October 1917), which overthrew Kerensky, the new government of Lenin and his Bolsheviks agreed to continue upgrading the railway with the help of the RRSC. This was in spite of the fact that the new government was seeking to opt out of the war.

The first batch of men representing the RRSC arrived in Vladivostok in December 1917 to find the port in turmoil. The Bolsheviks were now in control in Petrograd, 6000 miles to the west, and the situation in Siberia was confusing due to widespread lawlessness. Fortunately, Russian officials in Harbin (Chinese Manchuria) and the Bolshevik regime gave permission for members of the RRSC to begin work along the Chinese or Manchurian section of the railway.

The Czech Legion

The Czech Legion. At one stage it controlled 2500 miles of railway line from the Volga to Lake Baikal. The men lived in converted box cars with women they had picked up.
Within their trams they had a bank, post office and printing press, which produced a daily paper.
I have no idea how the mail got through. (Time Life)

Following the outbreak of World War I, ethnic Czechs and Slovaks within the Russian Empire petitioned Tsar Nicholas II to allow them to set up a national force to fight Austria, Hungary and Germany. The Tsar didn't give his consent until 1916, by which time the numbers applying to join the legion had increased enormously due to applications from Czech prisoners of war and deserters from the Austro-Hungarian Army (mainly Bohemians and Slovakians).

The leader and main driving force was Tomas Masaryk (a writer and political philosopher – later first president of Czechoslovakia). Under his direction the legion peaked at 65,000 men and, even throughout the disintegration of the Russian armies in 1917 and 1918, the legion remained a relatively coherent and disciplined force with a leaning towards the Tsar and a determination to continue fighting Austria, Hungary and Germany.

Following the October revolution (the overthrow of Kerensky and the Bolshevik take over) and the determination of the new Bolshevik government to seek peace with Germany, the Czech legion expressed a desire to continue fighting the Germans if necessary on Europe's western front (i.e. France). As the only feasible way to transfer the legion to France was by train across Siberia to the Pacific and then by ship to France, Masaryk obtained permission from the Soviet government for free passage via the railway to Vladivostok; permission was given, provided all legionaries handed over their weapons. Many did not. A shortage of rolling stock and poor maintenance along the line led to long delays, and by mid-May 1918, only 15,000 legionaries had reached Vladivostok.

Simultaneously, with the movement east of legionnaires, there was a transfer west along the line from Siberia of Hungarian prisoners of war (as agreed to by the treaty of Brest-Litovsk) for repatriation. On 14 May 1918 at Chelyabinsk Station, a train load of Czech legionnaires heading east came alongside a train load of Hungarian prisoners of war heading west. Nationalistic antipathy flared and a piece of iron was thrown from the Hungarian train into the Czech train, killing a Czech soldier. The Czechs retaliated by lynching the man responsible. The Chelyabinsk authority immediately stepped in and arrested a number of Czech soldiers and placed them in gaol. The legionnaires rose as a body and seized the local arsenal, forcibly released the prisoners and occupied the whole city.

Leon Trotsky, now the people's commissioner of war, ordered his force, the Red Army, to disarm all Czech legionaries and shoot on the spot any that refused to hand over their arms. This order proved impossible to implement for within two weeks most of the railway line from the Volga to Lake Baikal, a distance of 2500 miles, lay in the hands of either the Czechs or anti-Bolshevik forces.

Although mildly sympathetic to the Tsar, Masaryk did not want the legion to become embroiled in Russia's civil war, but was frustrated by the continued delays along the Trans-Siberian Railway. These delays, however, were suddenly overcome when the legion captured eight train carriages carrying gold bullion from the imperial reserve in Kazan. Now the Bolsheviks had to negotiate a deal: no more talk of giving up arms; no more shooting on sight, but a quick and safe passage to Vladivostok. The deal was completed in 1920.

Seven carriages of treasure were returned to the Russian government; the legion kept the eighth car so as to be able to lease ships in Vladivostok and to establish the Legion Bank in Prague, the capital of the newly formed state of Czechoslovakia.

Following the signing of the treaty of Brest-Litovsk between Russia and Germany in March 1918, the Russian Civil War broke out and inevitably the men of the RRSC became embroiled in the conflict between the Red Army, Czech legionaries, White Russians (monarchists) and even opportunistic warlords. To keep rail traffic moving under such chaotic conditions was a formidable task.

There seems little doubt that the RRSC brought about many improvements in the railway. It also seems that they tended to work closely with forces hostile to the soviets. They helped men of the Czech legion evacuate via Vladivostok and Admiral Kolchaks army to escape east from the advancing Red Army during the summer of 1919. But probably its greatest achievement was to keep the line open so that millions of non-Bolsheviks could escape to Manchuria and Japan.

The Siberian tiger. These animals, the largest of all the cats,
terrified workers on the eastern section of the line.

CHAPTER 16

HARBIN

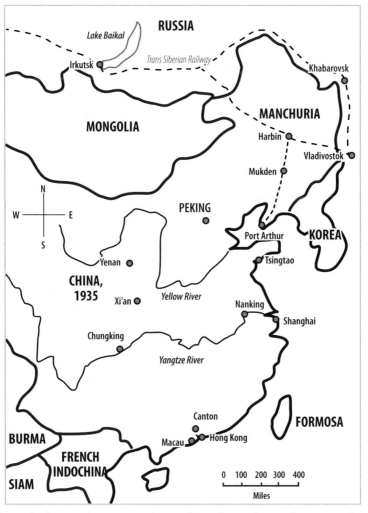

The author's map showing Harbin and its relationship to the Trans-Siberian,
Chinese Eastern (Manchurian) and Southern Manchurian railways.

I n 1896 Russia obtained from China a long term concession to build and operate a railway across Manchuria connecting the main Trans-Siberian line near Chita to Vladivostok on the Pacific coast. Three years later in 1898, Russia obtained a 25-year leasehold on the Liaotung Peninsula (containing Port Arthur) and permission to connect this leasehold to the main Manchurian line, now referred to as the Chinese Eastern and Southern Manchurian lines.

For such a large undertaking, Russia selected Harbin, a collection of small farm villages on the Songhua River within Chinese Manchuria, as the main construction and administrative base for both the eastern and southern lines. The Chinese also agreed that an area of twenty-five miles on either side of the line and seventy-five miles beyond certain centres be classified as Russian 'zones of influence' (including Harbin, Port Arthur, Mukden and Diarin). Within these zones of influence, Russians were granted extra-territorial rights, meaning citizens within these areas were subject to Russian, not Chinese, law and authority; they even had their own police force, hospitals, churches, schools and civil administrators.

Within a few years the new and relatively small railway town of Harbin was to develop into a well to do cultural conscious community with an ever growing and ambitious Russian population, which soon superseded the indigenous Chinese and Manchu.

Following the Russian defeat at the hands of the Japanese in 1905, all Russian rights in southern Manchuria were taken over by the Japanese. But Harbin and the Chinese eastern line remained in the hands of the Chinese and continued to be maintained and administered by the Russians. Harbin continued to prosper.

Twenty years later, as a result of the Russian revolutions and the subsequent civil war, hundreds of thousands of White Russians (monarchists) fled across the border into Manchuria (Chinese territory), and by 1918 the Russian population of Harbin had increased to over 200,000. This led to great developments within the city in spite of the fact that the Harbin administrators (and refugees) were with some justification considered by the Bolsheviks to be enemies.

Following the Bolshevik takeover in Russia, Russians living in

Harbin were told to choose either Chinese or Soviet citizenship as their current Russian passports were no longer valid, meaning these Russians were in fact now stateless. Those who chose to remain Russian citizens were ordered to return to Russia, where many were shot, sent to the Siberian Gulags or recruited as spies.

In 1918 the administration of the railway and Harbin officially reverted to the Chinese. The special zones were abolished, but Russian expertise in running the area, now without extra-territorial rights, left the Chinese with no choice but to keep the many now stateless Russians in charge. The Japanese remained protectors of the Southern Railway.

The ongoing chaos and disintegration in China resulted in Manchuria falling into the hands of a warlord Zhang Zuolin, the 'Old Marshall', who did business with the Japanese, who by treaty controlled the Southern Railway and the Liaotung Peninsula, but in northern Manchuria for political convenience he acknowledged Chinese authority. In Harbin, which is in Chinese Manchuria, the large White Russian population were theoretically free of Moscow's control and they continued to be employed to maintain the railway. Some moved to China proper and in particular to Shanghai. Some managed to move overseas to America, Canada or Australia but as they were in fact stateless without valid passports this was difficult and many remained in Harbin. These talented Russian expatriates built and staffed additional hospitals, schools, orthodox churches and chapels in contradistinction to the official atheist line taken by the communist government nearly 6000 miles away in Moscow.

In 1928, the Manchurian warlord Zhang Zuolin was killed in a railway accident (engineered by the Japanese) and was succeeded by his son the 'Young Marshall' who proved equally adept at dealing with the Japanese and Chiang Kai-shek's Government in China. He even managed to extend the railway system with Japanese money and retain Russian expertise.

During the 1920s, Harbin remained a vibrant and gay city, where it is said one could dance with a Russian countess for fifty cents in Mexican currency (the two warlords printed their own currency) or a younger member of the Russian nobility (it was remarkable how many, now free of Russian control, claimed connections with the imperial family) for an additional bottle of champagne, and for a little more money, you could even spend the night with a duchess after first dining on such culinary exotica as grilled bear's claw, deer nostrils and Siberian tiger testicles.

In 1931, Japan resigned from the League of Nations (the first nation to do so); the Japanese Army occupied the whole of Manchuria including Harbin and installed the last Chinese emperor (Puyi, a Manchu) as puppet head of state. They renamed Manchuria 'Manchukuo' and remained till defeated in 1945, when the area was briefly occupied by Russian troops, before being returned to communist China.

Although Russians still had a presence in Harbin after the Japanese takeover in 1932, the city became progressively industrialised and in 1949 well and truly under the control of communist China. No more warlords, no more dancing with grand duchesses and no more grilled bear's claws.

PART SIX

WAR'S END, 1917–1918

CHAPTER 17

Hong Kong

The Jewel of the Empire

During the 1830s the Emperor of China ruled in Peking. He issued edicts with a vermillion brush and exhorted foreign merchants to 'tremble and obey'. He had littler time for goods manufactured by outside barbarians entering the Middle Kingdom.

All this quickly changed when scarlet-uniformed troops over-powered Chinese forts and British warships sank imperial naval junks that went down with canons firing and gongs clanging. One of the results of British victories was that the fever-infested island of Hong Kong with one of the finest harbours in the world became a British colony.

Since its traumatic beginnings British Hong Kong has always lured an entrepreneurial breed of men and women determined to make their mark on life. Some returned to their native land with fortunes, some ended up as paupers and some settled to work out their days to finally rest in peace beneath a head stone in the old colonial cemetery near Happy Valley.

Much, much later, long after the emperor had gone, a document was signed in Peking's Great Hall of the People, by the Chinese and British prime ministers (1984), agreeing with the return of Hong Kong to China in 1997.

What had once been a malaria-infested island, the haunt of pirates and smugglers, had been transformed under British rule to become the showcase of capitalism, and then quite incredibly returned peacefully and in fine shape to communist China after 155 years of colonial rule.

Reference: Trea Wiltshire, *Hong Kong: The Last Prize of Empire* (Hong Kong, Asia Books, 4th edn, 1997).

O ur firm had arranged accommodation for me at Queen's Gardens, an attractive place half-way up the peak with a view over one of the finest harbours in the world.

When I arrived in Hong Kong in 1916 it was a peaceful haven; the war was raging but it was thousands of miles away. The Japanese were then our allies and had taken Tsingtao from the Germans, depriving them of a valuable naval base.

A few warships came and went, German raiders were said to be prowling the area but it seemed not to affect us. Travelling between Europe and the east by sea was particularly non-existent but we still received our mail from Europe, although greatly delayed, uncertain and severely censored.

My firm was chiefly engaged in the coastal shipping trade from Japan to the Dutch East Indies (Indonesia), Siam (Thailand), China and the Strait settlements (Malaysia and Singapore), which proved to be viable and profitable.

In spite of all the horrors in Europe, Russia and the Atlantic, our domestic life in Hong Kong continued undisturbed; our servant boys looked after our household needs, our social life was to us newcomers (referred locally as Griffins) centred around the Hong Kong Club, where one could tiffin and dine, play snooker, bridge or simply browse in a good library. Across the street were the Cricket Club and a number of tennis courts. The Yacht Club, Golf Club and Jockey Club were for later when one was more affluent.

During 1917 the news from Europe was not good. The U-boats were causing havoc. A war of attrition had evolved across southern Belgium and France, and on Germany's eastern front the Russians, after suffering huge losses, had forced the Tsar to abdicate and although Kerensky's provincial government had vowed to continue fighting, they were only to last till October 1917 when the Bolsheviks took over and made peace with Germany.

Hong Kong being primarily a shipping centre, we perhaps gave the war at sea more of our thoughts than the land fighting. Ships to us were almost living creatures and the submarine war of 1916–1917 took a tremendous toll of ships we knew and their officers, whom we had personally dealt with; sadly, many lost their lives.

But there were signs that the slaughter was coming to an end. Sheer exhaustion and wastage was telling, and the U-boat lost its potential when the convey system was introduced in 1917 and gradually took effect.

In the latter part of 1918 there was a feeling in the air that peace was near. On 11 November, I went down to the office rather early to see what the news might be. One of our skippers met me at the door with, 'It is all over, Sverre; they have signed the peace.' His ship was over at Stonecutter Island and he had been given a lift ashore in a pinnace by a naval signaller, who had told him it was all official.

My thoughts immediately went back to that little party on the Western Road, Glasgow, when we had listened to the midnight call of the newspaper boy that war had broken out. It had been a long time. A lot had happened to the world since then, and a bit of water had also flowed under my bridge.

The news soon spread, specials came out, and soon the rejoicings took over. Celebrations got underway; the Hong Kong Hotel was packed before the early morning cleaners got out. I'm afraid there wasn't much work done that day or even that week. An official bank holiday with thanksgiving was proclaimed: the Chinese, who can always be relied on for a celebration, staged a real slap-up dragon festival; fire crackers appeared by the mile, and walking through the city streets at times was a hazardous undertaking. Flags were flying everywhere; the ships in the harbour were all dressed up. The north-east monsoon had just put in an appearance and the bright sunshine added its golden blessing to the scene.

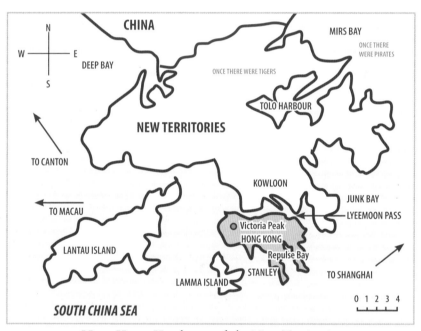

Hong Kong, Kowloon and the New Territories

CHAPTER 18

THE LAST TSAR

'No more separation, at last united for life, and when this life is ended we meet again in the other world to remain together for all eternity. Yours, yours.'
– From Nicki's diary, but in Alix's handwriting, on their wedding day, 27 November 1894

Tsar Nicholas II of Russia

During 1917 and 1918 the news from Russia and the executions of the imperial Russian family shocked the civilised world. This is how and why it happened.

In 1864 Princess Dagmar of Schleswig-Holstein, a member of the somewhat impoverished but noble Danish Glucksburg family (her elder sister Princess Alexandria married the Prince of Wales, later Edward VII) was only sixteen when she met her 'Dream Prince' the Tsarovich Nicholas of Russia. They were soon engaged but unfortunately in 1865 Nicholas, heir to the Russian throne, developed meningitis and died.

Fortunately Dagmar had a secret admirer, the younger brother of Nicholas, Grand Duke Alexander Alexandrovich, now heir to the throne. Quite surprisingly, Nicholas on his death bed expressed the wish that his bride to be would agree to marry his successor; even more surprisingly, Dagmar agreed to do so and it proved a loving marriage.

Dagmar adopted the Orthodox religion (she was brought up a Lutheran), taught herself Russian and changed her name to Marie Feodorovna. She was vivacious, attractive and soon became the leader of fashion in St Petersburg society. She threw glittering parties, was a very popular princess and later empress. Her husband, Alexander III, was a big man and bore little resemblance to his soft-hearted and impressionable father (who was assassinated), nor to their eldest son and heir, Nicholas, who truly believed that the Tsar was appointed by God and thus a divinely inspired source of wisdom and order. Alexander, however, believed that his son (the Tsar to be) was not even suited to sit on any worthwhile committees. This unfortunately was the man destined to rule Russia.

Dagmar, being Danish, had developed an abiding hatred for Bismarck and Prussia which had subjugated her country, Schleswig-Holstein, so that when her son and heir to the throne of Russia, Tsarovich Nicholas asked his parents for permission to marry Princess Alexandra (Alix) of Hesse and Rhine, a German principality, she opposed her son's wishes, for she feared the arrival of this German princess. In retrospect her fears were well founded. Nicholas nevertheless insisted on his choice, and Alix, who was also the grand daughter of Queen Victoria of England, and, unbeknown to all, carrying the defective sex-linked haemophiliac gene, became engaged to Nicholas in April 1894. Alexander III died in November that year, and Nicholas became Tsar at the age of twenty-six.

Alix of Hesse accompanied the imperial family on their return to St Petersburg with the body of the tsar. It is said that the people greeted their new empress to be with ominous whispers, 'She comes to us behind a coffin.' Shortly after the funeral, they were married on 26 November 1894 at the Winter Palace in St Petersburg and Alix became Empress of Russia.

Alix, who like her husband was deeply religious, had not an ounce of frivolity or charm in her make up; she nevertheless came to dominate her husband (who adored her), both in family and political matters and was not at all popular with other members of the royal household, including her mother-in-law. This deep rift within the Russian royal family was to contribute to the instability in Russia.

Nicholas, a kindly, religious little man, was ill-equipped to cope with the increasing unrest in his vast empire especially following Russia's defeat in the war with Japan (1904–1905).

Bloody Sunday

Father George Gapon, a somewhat mysterious figure, an orthodox priest, an organiser of the union of Russian factory workers and self appointed representative of the underprivileged of St Petersburg had requested Tsar Nicholas II to meet his subjects, the poor of the city, in the Winter Palace square at two o'clock on Sunday 22 January 1905, in order to hear their grievances.

It was understood that the tsar had agreed to this request. A petition had previously been sent to the 'little father' and signed by 135,000 of his subjects suggesting modest reform.

So they gathered together in the freezing weather and shuffled peacefully with good intent towards the Winter Palace. Some carried icons; others portraits of the tsar; some had with them their wives and children. As they walked, they sang hymns. It had been a great effort to get them all together but they did so want to present their petition to the tsar so that he could redress the injustices foisted on them by the corrupt capitalists and bureaucrats.

When they arrived at the square they learnt that the tsar was not there. They were unaware that the tsar had been advised not to attend, for he nearly had an accident two days before,

> which some believed was an unsuccessful attempt on his life.
>
> Instead of the tsar there were ranks of soldiers. They, the poor of St Petersburg who had made this great effort in freezing weather, were ordered to leave. And when they hesitated, a bugle sounded, the soldiers fired on them and then the Cossacks rode them down.
>
> That was the heartless massacre of 'Bloody Sunday', which effectively put a stop to any faith the silent masses might have had in the tsar. From now on, everything would be different.
>
> Philip Guedalla, *The Hundred Years* (London, Hodder & Stoughton, 1937).

Alix, after having four daughters, at last produced a son, Alexei. Unfortunately and unbeknown to all, she had passed on to her son the defective haemophiliac gene, which she had inherited from her mother, who had in turn inherited it from her mother, Queen Victoria. Haemophilia is due to a sex-linked gene; if present it may be carried by females who are unaffected but may pass it on to a son, resulting in the inability of his blood to clot, so that profuse bleeding occurs following any minor trauma.

Nicholas and Alix decided to keep their son's disease secret, robbing the royal family of the understanding and compassion of the Russian people; and as the imperial couple's life became more secluded and secretive, rumours spread about the child's affliction. Much worse was to follow when a mysterious monk, Rasputin, a peasant claiming mystical powers that could be utilised to cure every illness, was recommended to the empress and accepted by her into the imperial household in the hope that he would cure her son. The acceptance of Rasputin, who already had an evil reputation, was very much against the advice of the tsar's mother and led to further gossip and rumours of sexual improprieties.

In spite of further advice from his mother, Nicholas would not banish Rasputin nor his influence from the imperial household. However, in the winter of 1916, a group of nobles took matters into their own hands. They invited Rasputin to dinner (which flattered him immensely), where they murdered him and placed his body under the ice of a canal just off the River Neva. The body, however, was found, and, at the insistence of the empress, a burial service was held. The tsar returned from the front to attend and Rasputin's body was laid to rest beneath the Royal Chapel at Tsarskoye Selo. Some say that this act was the first step towards the 1917 revolution.

Sankt Petersburg

In 1698, Peter the Great returned to Russia after two years abroad, determined to Europeanise Russians and expand his empire. He first set about building two navies, one to attack the Turks in the south and the other to attack the Swedes in the north.

At that time Russia's only access to the sea was its Arctic coast, where the waters were frozen during most of the year, so his ships had to be built on rivers. In 1703 he defeated the Swedes and captured a stretch of coast on the Gulf of Finland. To protect his newly acquired territory from Swedish reprisals, he ordered the construction of a fortress on a broad marsh at the mouth of the Neva River. This was called the Peter and Paul Fortress.

From this fortress, Peter set about building a European city. The principal architect was from Switzerland. Labour was conscripted. All nobles owning more than thirty families of serfs (forced labourers) were ordered to build houses in the new city; while those owning more than five hundred serfs had to build stone houses of at least two storeys. It all cost 200,000 lives, mostly from fever and exposure; but no city grew more quickly, and by 1712, Sankt Petersburg was proclaimed capital of all Russia and so it remained for 206 years.

For patriotic reasons the city's name was changed to the more Russian-sounding name, Petrograd, in 1914, by which time the city had grown into one of Europe's most magnificent capitals. In 1918 following the revolution, Petrograd lost its pre-eminence as Russia's capital to Moscow, a city founded as a military outpost against the tartars (central Asian tribes) in 1147. In 1924, the city's name, Petrograd, was changed yet again to Leningrad in memory of the father of the revolution.

Finally in 1991 with the collapse of the Soviet Union, a citizens' referendum decided quite correctly to reinstate the city's original name, Sankt Petersburg, and so it remains today.

Reference: Geraldine Norman, *The Hermitage* (London, Jonathan Cape, 1994).
Norman Davies, *Europe* (London, Pimlico, 1997).

In 1914 Russia entered World War I on the side of Britain and France. She faced Germany and Austria and in spite of her huge army, it very soon became apparent that she did not have the technical ability to fight a modern war.

The tsar (who regarded it to be his God-like duty) from his military headquarters near the front sought to carry out the duties of a sovereign to lead and direct his armies, but his armies seemed incapable of defeating the enemy. The tragic figures were immense – by 1917, two million Russians dead and four million wounded – and what had they to show for it? An invaded country, the prospect of further defeats by German metal and continual privations at home because of sheer incompetence.

In Petrograd, there were strikes and lockouts, the workers were underfed, and the Cossacks sent to control them soon sided with them for they too were underfed.

On Monday 12 March 1917, three regiments of guards stationed in Petrograd mutinied, and the dumas (which passed for a parliament) acted by forming a provisional government.

That night, the tsar started home by train from the front, but the track was blocked by mutineers. They all wanted him to abdicate; Petrograd, the tsar's advisors and his army commanders telegraphed him to do so; someone from Petrograd was already on the way in a single carriage train to show him how it could be done. On 15 March 1917, the tsar in this railway carriage at the Pskov siding west of the capital abdicated. Before signing the papers, he asked his doctor if his son was curable. When the doctor shook his head, Nicholas signed on behalf of himself and his son. Tsar Nicholas abdicated in favour of his brother Michael; but as a Romanov, Michael was not acceptable and he abdicated immediately. The abdication of the tsar and the establishment of a provisional government marked the first Russian revolution.

Russia was now a republic ruled by a government soon dominated by Kerensky, a Menshevik (leftish socialist), who nevertheless was prepared to fight on against Germany and Austria.

Immediately after abdicating, Nicholas was allowed to return to the front and on 20 March he addressed the soldiers, extolling them to be loyal to the provisional government and to continue the war against Germany and Austria. He was then allowed to return to Petrograd to be confined with his family in the palace Tsarskoye Selo.

There was the vague hope that they would soon be off to exile in England but this was delayed, partly because of some reticence on behalf of the British government, partly because the children had measles and partly because Karensky had second thoughts. Perhaps it would be better to keep them in Russia so that Karensky's government could keep a close eye on them. The Bolshevik minority wanted the whole family tried for murder and treason.

Although the tsar had abdicated, Karensky's government decided to continue the war against Germany and Austria. In this he had the support of the Mensheviks, all right wing elements in Russia and of course the Western allies. The Bolsheviks, however, were opposed to any further fighting and wished to sue for peace. The German high command to support the Bolsheviks and to further destabilise the situation in Russia arranged to transfer Lenin from Switzerland to Russia via Germany and Sweden.

Map of Germany's and Austria-Hungary's eastern front, showing the extent of their adavnce when Russia collapsed towards the end of 1917. At the treaty of Brest-Litovsk, Russia lost thirty-two percent of its agricultural land.

Lenin 1870–1924

Vladimir Ilych Ulyanov, better known by his pseudonym Lenin, became a Marxist after his brother was executed in 1887 for attempting to assassinate Tsar Alexander III. In 1898, he joined other Marxist groups to form the Russian Democratic Workers' Party.

The party split in 1903 over Lenin's concepts of a more radical Bolshevik party that envisaged the overthrow of the government and the setting up of a Soviet state with a supreme chairman, a virtual dictatorship. The less radical Mensheviks, although favouring the overthrow of the tsar, believed in a more loosely knit and democratic government.

Lenin became an active revolutionary and was exiled to Siberia where he married another Marxist, Nadezhda Drupskaya. After serving out his time he returned to Russia. Later, following the failure of the 1905 uprising, Lenin fled into exile and settled in Switzerland.

Following the first Russian revolution in 1917, Lenin returned to Russia with the assistance of the German government. He called for the replacement of Kerensky's Menshevik-dominated provisional government and peace with Germany. But initially Lenin did not have the numbers and was forced to flee yet again, this time across the border to Finland.

When Kerensky's government failed seven months later, Lenin returned in October 1917 to successfully lead the Bolsheviks to power. This was the second revolution. Lenin immediately set up the Soviet of People's Commissars under his chairmanship. He then made peace with Germany and led the revolutionaries to victory in the Russian Civil War (1918–1920), ruthlessly crushing any opposition. He initiated far-reaching social reforms and advocated world communism.

In 1922, an unsuccessful attempt was made on Lenin's life and, shortly after, he began to experience a number of strokes. He died in 1924.

To continue fighting, the Russian army required reorganisation and massive supplies. Because of the inadequacies of Russian industries, these supplies would have to come from abroad; and, because German U-boats prevented any supplies reaching Russia from the West, supplies had to be brought in from the Pacific (i.e. America) and transhipped to Russia's western front via the Trans-Siberian Railway, a distance of 6000 miles from Vladivostok, a truly gigantic logistic problem.

Karensky asked for help to upgrade the recently completed line and improve efficiency. This help came from America with the formation of the Russian Railway Service Corporation.

The provisional government lasted seven months, through spring and summer, during which time unrest continued as did military defeats.

On the night of 25 October 1917, according to the Julian calendar (6-7 November, Gregorian calendar), the Petrograd garrison and sailors from Kronstadt seized government offices and stormed the Winter Palace. Kerensky fled abroad and Lenin formed a new government, which immediately made peace overtures with Germany. This was Russia's second revolution.

On 15 December 1917, agreement was reached with Germany for a 28-day truce effective from 17 December. The formal treaty of Brest-Litovsk (German army HQ in Poland) was signed on 3 March 1918. Russia immediately lost thirty-two percent of its agriculture land; Finland, Ukraine and Georgia became independent states, while Poland, Estonia and Lithuania became part of the German Empire (albeit temporarily). This was a harsh peace, but the irony of Brest-Litovsk for Germany was that far from liberating all German troops for redeployment to her western front, nearly a million men had to be retained in eastern Europe to hold her newly acquired territory.

Russia now entered into a period of instability and civil war, which was to cause the loss of more lives and misery than had the war with Germany and Austria.

While still in power, Kerensky had arranged the transfer of the former tsar and his family to Tobolsk, a small town in western Siberia. Before the tsar left Petrograd, Kerensky is reported to have told him, 'The Bolsheviks are after me and when they have me they will come for you.' Although under guard, the tsar and his family were comfortable in Tobolsk. Local inhabitants continued to show great respect, removing their caps and crossing themselves when passing the mansion where the imperial family was being held. It was a pro-tsarist town.

In May 1918, the Bolshevik (Soviet) government ordered that the tsar and his family be transferred to Ekaterinburg (Yekaterinburg) a pro-Bolshevik town where the citizens did not doff their hats or cross themselves in respect. But the Soviets had a new problem. The Russian white armies containing units of the Czech legion were advancing on Ekaterinburg; indeed, citizens of the town and the royal prisoners could hear the gunfire. The local Bolsheviks asked Moscow what they should do with the imperial family. It would appear that the answer was, 'Take your own measures.'

On the night of 16 July, factory worker guards about the tsar's residence were replaced by cheka executioners, Lenin's brutal force formed to deal with counter-revolutionaries. There were to be twelve executioners. In the early hours of the morning of 17 July, they entered the Patlev house where the tsar and his family were held prisoners. Yurovsky, their leader, woke the family doctor (Dr Boticin) and informed him, 'In view of the unrest in the town, it would be dangerous to remain upstairs in the bedrooms, and the whole Romanov family must move to the basement.' Doctor Boticin then woke the family. The Romanovs slowly dressed and were led to the cellar room. The tsar carried his son; the maid and the girls carried pillows. Two chairs were placed in the room, one for the empress and one for Alexei.

Yurovsky to their great surprise then read the sentence: 'In view of the fact that your relatives are continuing their attack on Soviet Russia, the Ural Executive Committee has decided to execute you.' The Romanovs were stunned; the tsar appeared not to hear the sentence clearly, so it was read again. The last words the tsar uttered were, 'You know not what you do.' The executioners opened fire; it was not well done. The tsar died immediately; all executioners wanted to kill him. The empress died sitting in the chair, but the three daughters did not die quickly; bullets ricocheted off their corsets or buried themselves in pillows. Little Alexei, wounded, crawled along the floor putting his hand up in a pathetic effort to shield himself from the bullets. Eventually they stopped but Demidova the maid was still alive, running to and fro, screaming. The executioners chased after her with bayonets; one she grasped with both hands in a vain attempt to prevent it entering her chest. Both the doctor and dog were shot.

The bodies were carried to a waiting lorry. When being laid on a stretcher, one of the daughters cried out, rose and covered her face with her arm. Then another 'slain' grand duchess suddenly rose up and screamed. Horror gripped the drivers and helpers; to some of them this 'strange vitality' suggested that heaven itself was against them. The twelve chekas did not err; heaven did not worry them. They took their bayonets and stabbed all the bodies again. Such was the style of the paid servants of the disciples of the new messiah Karl Marx.

They drove to the burial site. The bodies were undressed. Jewels were found sewn in the women's corsets and each of the girls was noted to have a picture of Rasputin hanging from a necklace around her neck. The clothes were burnt and the bodies thrown down a shallow mine shaft.

Kolchak units(White Russian and Czech legionnaires) entered Eka-terinburg five days after the murders.

Hymns from the Earth

Less than twenty-four hours after the execution of the tsar and his family, more Romanovs and their entourage were murdered, including the beautiful but tragic grand duchess, Elizaveta Feodorovna, the elder sister of the now murdered empress.

Ella, as she was known to the family, had married the younger brother of Alexander III and was therefore Nicholas' aunt and sister-in-law. Her husband, Grand Duke Sergei, was homosexual. He was assassinated in 1905, and Ella was left childless and without a husband. She sought comfort in the Orthodox church and even established convents.

Elizaveta seemed almost to be seeking martyrdom; even knowing her life was in danger from the Bolsheviks, she turned down all offers of security and escape even from the German Kaiser (who had once wooed her).

Following the second revolution, Elizaveta and five of her companions including other members of the imperial household were imprisoned in a disused school building. They were condemned to death by the Bolsheviks and on the night of 17 July the official assassins decided to carry out their sentence.

I précis the report presented by the chief assassin Ryabov:

On the night of 17 July 1918, the six victims were taken from the school building where they had been held. They were blindfolded and driven to a disused mine shaft.

First we threw the grand duchess down the shaft. We heard her struggling in the water at the bottom of the shaft for some time. We next pushed the nun down after her. We heard the splash and then the two women's voices. We then threw the men down the shaft. We could still hear voices, so we threw two grenades down the shaft. Then, from beneath the ground, we heard singing. I was seized with horror; they were singing the prayer 'Lord Save Your People'. We had no more hand grenades, so we filled the shaft with dry brushwood and set it alight. In spite of this, their hymns still rose up through the smoke for some time. So we left.

Over the next few days peasants working in the vicinity reported hearing hymns being sung from within the mine shaft. Later, when White Russian troops recaptured the area, they retrieved the bodies and found that a head wound on one of the victims had been bound up with the grand duchess' handkerchief.

Much, much later, the Orthodox Church declared Elizaveta a saint under the title Saint Elizaveta Feodorovna.

Reference: Andrei Maylunas and Sergei Mironenko, A Life Long Passion (London, Weidenfeld & Nocholson, 1996).

Many years later, following the fall of the communist dictatorship in Russia, Nicholas's bones were exhumed, their authenticity confirmed by DNA testing and reburied with those of his wife and children (except Anastasia, whose remains were never found) with due ceremony at St Petersburg with his forbears at the Peter and Paul Fortress. In 2000AD the Russian Orthodox Church declared Nicholas to be a true saint.

Following the first revolution, Dagmar moved to a villa in the Crimea and spent two years under house arrest before being rescued by the British battleship HMS *Marlborough* and taken to England to join her sister, Alexandra, the widow of King Edward VII. After a brief stay in England, she returned to Denmark where she remained till her death in 1928.

In 2005, the governments of Denmark and Russia agreed that the remains of the empress Her Serine Highness Princess Marie Sophie Frederikke Dagmar should be relocated to St Petersburg and laid to rest beside her loving husband Alexander III (said to be the only tsar who never took a mistress), seventy-seven years after her death.

The Calendar

In the year 980AD Grand Duke Vladimir became ruler of Kievan Russia. An excellent soldier and administrator he soon expanded his territory and by 1000AD, Kievan Russia was second in area in Europe to the Holy Roman Empire.

In 986AD Vladimir was approached by representatives of various faiths. He decided to embrace Christianity; but was it to be Rome or Byzantium? To assess their relative values, he sent emissaries to Rome and Byzantium. The emissaries were so impressed with the great cathedral, Hagia Sophia, in Byzantium (St Peters was not yet built) that they recommended Byzantium. This, together with Vladimir's refusal to accept the Roman pope's temporal authority, led him to decree that Byzantium, or the Greek Orthodox (Russian Orthodox) Church was to be the state religion.

Russians, having been converted into the Orthodox faith, decided to number the years according to biblical accounts. As the creation of the world occurred in the year 5509BC (according to the Orthodox faith) that year was year one. Furthermore, and to be consistent, each new year must begin in September, for that is the time that apples are ripe and available for serpents to tempt Eve. There are no apples on the trees in January in Russia.

Much later, Peter the Great in cooperation with the Orthodox Church decreed, against much opposition, that this must change and in future Russians must adopt the Julian Calender, which had been introduced by Julius Caesar in 45BC, but not the more up to date Gregorian calendar that superseded it in 1582AD.

By the twentieth century, the difference between the Julian and Gregorian calendar was thirteen days and in 1918, following the revolution, Lenin decreed that from henceforth Russia would adopt the Gregorian calendar. This meant that the dates for the two revolutions were 25 February and 25 October according to the Julian calendar and 8 March and 7 November according to the Gregorian calendar.

This was not to be the end of the matter and there was to be further tinkering. In 1929, the Soviets introduced the 'Eternal calendar', meaning five days a week and six weeks per month, after two years this was further changed to a six days per week calendar. At last, in 1940, the standard Gregorian calendar was reintroduced with seven days per week, just like the rest of the world.

CHAPTER 19

THE AFTERMATH

Lines of grey, muttering faces, masked with fear
They leave their trenches, going over the top
While time ticks blank and busy on their wrists
And hope, with furtive eyes and grappling fists,
Flounders in mud. O Jesus make it stop!
– Siegfried Sassoon

At 0400 hours on 21 March 1918, Germany mounted what was to be her final assault on the west. German troups attacked with great élan; early successes and the ferocity of the attacks caused near panic amongst the British and French High Command, but, although bent, the line held and by July the German offensive had slowed down and stalled.

On 17 July 1918, the French launched a massive counter stroke and on 8 August 1918, 430 tanks moved forwards in front of the advancing British Fourth Army. The German front began to cave in as the western allies rolled forward. In the following three months the British army alone took 180,000 prisoners.

An exhausted Germany had had enough. On 4 October 1918, the German and Austrian governments despatched notes to President Wilson asking for armistice negotiations to be opened. Political bargaining prolonged the war until the Germans, with their armies continually retreating and rising discontented at home, agreed to an unconditional surrender.

The German peace delegates left Spa (Belgium) on 7 November and crossed the frontier around 9 pm. The French put the delegates onto a train, which early next morning pulled into a siding in the forest of Compiègne, forty miles north of Paris.

At dawn on 8 November the German delegates were escorted to a nearby single carriage (carriage 2419D). Within this carriage negotiations began, while back in Germany revolution broke out, the Kaiser resigned and a new government was formed. On the evening of 10 November the German delegates were authorised to accept the armistice terms. They signed at 5 am on 11 November 1918. The guns fell silent six hours later; so ended 'the war to end wars'. Certainly for Britain, France, America, Germany and Austria the war was now over, but not in eastern Europe and Russia, where war, savagery and brutality continued.

Before all this happened, nature intervened, or perhaps an angry God, furious at man's continual folly placed a curse on all humankind. In early 1918 a strange form of influenza suddenly appeared in America and Western Europe. The disease affected mainly young people, and although extremely contagious it was not initially particularly lethal. Being contagious, the epidemic became prevalent in army camps where young men were herded together.

We can only speculate on the origins of the epidemic. Was it transferred to man from chickens and mutated to be passed from man to man? We really do not know. It is possible that the epidemic in its original milder form originated in America and American troops carried the virus to Europe.

In those days influenza was not known to be a viral disease; some blamed it on the planet Jupiter and its position in the heavens. Mussolini, dictator of Italy, claimed transmission was due to the dirty habit of handshaking and recommended the more hygienic Fascist salute. Whatever the truth, the fact is that within four months, and without the benefit of international flight, the virus had circled the globe. Then this initially fairly benign virus mutated into a far more lethal strain. They called it *la grippe* or the Spanish flu because Spanish newspapers (Spain was not involved in World War I) highlighted the problem instead of the events at the battle front.

It was not known then, but the virus responsible for Spanish flu initiated in young otherwise healthy people a catastrophic overreaction by a vigorous immune system. This over-reaction could at one extreme fill the lungs with fluid, antibodies, proteins and cells, making gaseous exchange almost impossible, resulting in many dying of respiratory failure. An American doctor at an army camp wrote in September 1918, 'It is only a matter of a few hours until death comes, and it is simply a struggle for air until they suffocate. It is horrible.'

More often, however, the reaction was not quite as severe. Instead, the virus so damaged the lining cells of the air passages that they were unable to resist any secondary bacterial invasion. The patient, then with a compromised immune system, developed a severe pneumonia, often with a pleural effusion (i.e. an acute empyema of the lung) or pus between the ribcage and underlying lung. Thousands of young people developed these conditions.

The medical profession was faced with an enormous problem. Doctors knew very little about overreactive immune systems. This was in the days before antibiotics or adequate cardiopulmonary support systems.

For acute empyema associated with Spanish flu, doctors initially utilised treatment recommended years before for chronic empyema (in reality a very different problem) and carried out open drainage to let the pus out of the pleural cavity. Open drainage entailed making an incision through the chest wall and leaving it open until all the pus had drained out. The results in the case of the Spanish flu were disastrous. In some American camp hospitals, open drainage led to a 70 percent mortality. An empyema commission was set up by the American government and as a result open drainage was discontinued. The mortality associated with acute empyema dropped to 5 percent.

The political consequences were enormous. Initially the magnitude of the problem was not recognised (except in Spain) for the war was at its height and took priority in the media and everyone's mind, but when the death rate due to this new disease began to rise, fear gripped the public. Troop ships were death ships, stories circulated in America that the plague was deliberately manufactured by the Germans and secretly released into their homeland via a submarine. Crowded troopships returning with soldiers brought the more virulent strain of the disease back to their homeland; 250,000 people died in England, 675,000 in America and in far away Australia 11,500 died of Spanish flu. Accurate figures for India are not available but it is estimated that 17 million died there. The streets of London were deserted, schools closed and people wore masks. The disease reached Hong Kong, Fiji and the Solomon Islands. It was the greatest acute pandemic of the twentieth century. It has been estimated that 3–5 percent of the total human population was affected by the pandemic.

For a time the Great War and its immediate aftermath was regarded as the greatest calamity of modern times. The war virtually ruined England. Great Britain entered the war as 'The World Banker' and at war's end she owed the US billions of pounds and her national debt had increased enormously.

The loss of British life far exceeded her death toll during World War II. Nearly one-tenth of all those that served were killed. In fact, England lost a generation, half a million men under the age of thirty – notably among them were junior officers who were expected to lead their men 'over the top' into battle and consequently were mowed down first. Proportionally, casualties among junior officers were three times higher than those amongst non-commissioned soldiers, they were called the lost generation (les sacrifiés). One-quarter of the Oxford and Cambridge students under the age of twenty-five who served in the British Army in 1914 were killed. In Kitchener's new army, all recruits with a private education were usually offered a commission. It was therefore these young men who suffered disproportionate casualties.

The French lost almost 20 percent of their men of military age and if we include the wounded and disabled not much more than one in three came through unscathed. Like the French and the British, the Germans and Russians sustained enormous losses.

The horrors of trench warfare on the western front were, however, to have a darker and more sinister effect than the horrific casualties. Many of those who survived trench warfare (on both sides) became incommunicable; some developed a savage sense of superiority both to women and those who had not served and some were to fill the ranks of the ultra right. On the eastern front the privations, inefficiencies and defeats led to unrest in Europe, instability, communism and eventually fascism.

Both sides tried to win by utilising new technology; poison gas, mines, massive artillery, armoured vehicles or tanks and the still frail aeroplanes but in truth, the only new technology which had a major effect on warfare in 1914–1918 was the submarine. Utilised to great effect by the Germans, the U-Boat came close to forcing the allies to sue for a negotiated peace. Unfortunately for Germany, unrestrained submarine warfare did more than anything else to bring America into the war and this was to prove decisive.

If all the sacrifices made by Britain during the 'Great War' were supposed to prevent Germany's occupation of continental Europe, the achievement was short lived, for within twenty years a far more serious German threat was to emerge and because of the cost of World War I (financially, psychologically and in lives) Britain was far worse placed to resist Germany's expansionist policies. From England's point of view, her involvement in World War I was a waste of blood and treasure, for in spite of Germany's naval program, which worried England during the early 1900's, Britain retained a substantial advantage and sooner or later Russia was bound to challenge Germany in a war of attrition.

Never in history had there been such an upheaval as the World War. Never had so many men died in battle or in the pandemic that followed. Down came the reigning houses of Europe, the Habsburgs, the Hohenzollerns, the Ottomans and last but not least the Romanovs of Russia.

It was in Russia that the greatest changes occurred. The tsars were replaced by a new breed of men, the Bolsheviks, followers of the new prophet, Karl Mark. These men, Lenin, Trotsky and Stalin, preached the communist manifesto not only in Russia but to the world at large and in their minds the goal must be achieved no matter what the cost in human life.

In truth, it was questionable whether the world was a much better place after 1918.

References: Eric Hobsbawn, *Age of Extremes* (Great Britain, Abacus, 1941).

Niall Ferguson, *Virtual History* (London, Picador, 1997).

Norman Davies, *Europe* (London, Pimlico, 1997).

Martin Gilbert, *The First World War* (London, Harper Collins, 1994).

Robert Massie, *Dreadnought* (London, Pimlico, 1993).

James McMillan, *The Way It Was, 1914–1934* (London, William Kimber, 1979).

Les Carlyon, *The Great War* (Sydney, Pan Macmillan, 2006).

Correlli Barnett, *The Sword Bearers* (London, Hodder & Stoughton, 1986).

PART SEVEN

CHINA, 1917–1941

CHAPTER 20

MARRIAGE AND THE VOYAGE HOME

Sverre and Connie, Hong Kong, 1921

With the end of the war, we in Hong Kong felt that a new and prosperous era was about to occur, a time to make up for lost opportunities; a flexing of financial muscle and expansion of business – and so it did – for a time.

As anticipated there was a great shortage of ships due to sinkings during the war and shipyards around the world were busy to meet the demand.

Our firm was well to the fore, as in addition to placing contracts for three China coasters we also had on the stocks two 8200 tonners, destined for the European trade. Many of these ships were now being built in Hong Kong and our first ship was due for completion in June 1921.

In 1921, I met a vivacious, artistic and attractive lady from Australia, Connie Hendry. We were married on 22 March 1922. She was one of four children brought up with her family in Adelaide. Connie was an event hostess on one of the cruise liners operating from Australia to the Far East (Philippines, Malaysia, Siam, Hong Kong, China and Japan). Connie could dance, paint and was so often the life of the party.

We took the opportunity to celebrate our marriage by taking my overdue home leave on 'our' new ship, skippered by a captain who was an old friend. She was basically a cargo ship but contained two really first class cabins and as another married couple, friends of ours, also found it convenient to go on leave, we looked forward to a wonderful voyage to Europe.

It was July and the heat was intense as we cast off and headed south. We were able to dodge a couple of typhoons and then thankfully experience a few days of fresh monsoon weather, which helped to cool us down. The captain took a course south of Singapore, Ceylon and India. We called at Aden for bunkers, where we did our duty by having drinks ashore near the parched palm trees in the town square.

It was extremely hot in our cabin as we steamed into the Red Sea. There were fans of course, but no air conditioning, so I arranged for Connie and me to sleep on stretchers placed on deck just below the bridge and outside the captain's cabin. I also arranged for our steward to deliver our early morning tea on deck, after which Connie and I would sit chatting while admiring the sea and sky and the sun rising out of Arabia on the start of its daily voyage across the heavens to Africa.

One morning while we were sipping our tea there was an agonising cry from the captain, 'Come quickly.' I rushed to his cabin to find him prancing about in his pyjamas with blood squirting all over the place from his penis, which he was holding with both hands. I called the mate and between us we attempted to stop the flow but it was not easy. We tried a tourniquet – not good; it all went black and blue. Finally we got it plugged with sticking plaster; it was not a pretty sight!

It was obvious that we would have to get the skipper to hospital so the ship was diverted to Port Sudan, the nearest place that had the facilities of a doctor and hospital. We landed the skipper late that afternoon; the doctor was on the wharf to meet us and whisked the skipper to hospital to be stitched up.

We of course investigated the cause of this disaster. It would appear that the steward had left the captain's cup of morning tea with a bottle of eau de cologne on the chair in front of his bed while he, the captain was still asleep. Getting out of bed and still a bit drowsy, the captain sat on the tea tray, the bottle broke and lacerated his penis and the hot tea spilt and scalded his penis, the result, a very painful and unholy mess and an unscheduled visit to Port Sudan.

Port Sudan on the African side of the Red Sea is an important cable station with a European staff who were in fact fairly isolated and longed for outside company to break the monotony of their lives. They were delighted to see us and we had quite a hilarious evening ashore as guests at their mess and of course the poor captain's problems occupied a lot of the conversation!

Next day we collected the captain and continued our voyage north to Port Suez, then through the canal to Port Said where the captain's stitches were removed and the traumatised organ pronounced as good as new, which is just as well as his wife unexpectedly turned up. The owners had kindly arranged a passage out for her from England as a surprise for the wounded captain. She was naturally surprised and wanted to know what he had been up to!

Our voyage ended at St Nazaire where the ship was to discharge her cargo. We had a gay farewell after which Connie and I took the train to Nantes, met up with and had a pleasant evening with Captain Lefevre and Madame Rollins whose husband had thankfully survived the war. Then by train up

Derek Berg

through Europe, a stopover at Copenhagen (which we loved), then by ferry to Oslo where I had the obligatory meeting with our directors, finally by train to Trondheim and a happy reunion with my parents who were delighted with Connie.

Trondheim is a very old city with old houses and old institutions. Although it is interesting, I was disappointed and felt that a few modern changes were needed; perhaps I had grown away from the apron strings having worked abroad for nearly ten years.

Nidaros

During the eighth century a number of Norse families settled and established themselves in the fertile region about the Trondheim Fjord (the Trondalag).

Hakon Grjotgardson became undisputed ruler of the whole region and quite coincidentally further south a Viking, Harold Fairhare was also carving out a kingdom for himself and with great foresight married Hakon's daughter and by agreement became Norway's first king. Harold was succeeded by his son, Hakon the Good, who decided to rule the country from the Trondalag.

Hakon The Good's reign was short. He was defeated by Danish Vikings and Norway fell under the rule of the Danish king. Then in 995AD another Viking, Olaf Tryggvason, on returning to Norway from England with a fleet of battle-hardened Vikings and meeting little opposition, advanced onto the Trondalag and was pronounced king by the Norwegian Parliament (his statue towers over Tronheim's town centre). Olaf had the port town Nidaros built (Trondheim) and ordered what was to be the largest longboat ever built – 160 feet long, propelled by thirty-four pairs of oars and a huge rectangular sail seventy feet across made of double layered coarse wool for strength and durability.

Olaf's reign, like Hakon's, was short. He too was defeated and killed by a combination of Danes and Swedes, so that Norway again became a Danish colony.

There was, however, another Olav, the great, great grandson of Harold Fairhare, who like Olaf Tryggvason reclaimed Norway, rebuilt Nidaros and set about making Norway a Christian country. His name was Olaf Haraldsson. Sadly, he too was defeated and killed in battle.

Olaf Haraldsson was a good man and shortly after his death was canonised. Later, construction began on what was to become the finest building in the whole of Scandinavia, Nidaros Cathedral, and for centuries thereafter pilgrims from all over Europe visited the cathedral to pray and renew their strength. Trondheim remained Norway's Christian capital until 1299 when the centre of government was moved to Oslo.

It was an awful shock to me to find that Norway had gone dry and joined the prohibition scramble pushed by a surfeit of do-gooders, especially in the USA. Fortunately there are always means of getting over stupid obstacles. The medical profession certainly had a field day diagnosing fictitious diseases requiring alcohol and writing prescriptions at five kroners per prescription for essential bottles of alcohol. My parents who have never been drinkers were quite shocked when I collected many prescriptions and laid in what I regarded as a reasonable supply for myself, Connie and friends. When we went to a restaurant we had to take our booze in a handbag and drink the brew out of tea cups; believe you me, it never tastes the same.

We were, however, fortunate with the weather, an unexpected taste of winter in October with plenty of snow and the opportunity to introduce Connie to skiing.

Long before I went abroad in 1913, a group of us had formed a small sporting club with no more than a dozen members. Surprisingly this club was still in existence and they welcomed me with open arms. As a result we all had some wonderful skiing in a valley not far from Trondheim where we as boys used to hire a farmhouse, which was still available. Those days skiing were the best part of our home leave.

All good things come to an end and time was running out, so I had to make plans for our return trip to Hong Kong. Head office kindly arranged a double cabin on a Japanese cargo / passenger liner and with a packed ship we set sail.

We were a mixed crowd, most of us returning from leave and of course short of money. The bar steward who had been on the run before understood the problem and accepted chits, the debt being paid once we reached our destination. There were of course a few newcomers on board, with optimistic expectations to make their pot of gold in the orient.

We had a pleasant trip, called at the usual ports, Port Said, Aden, Colombo, Singapore and finally Hong Kong. The passengers were a friendly lot and it was not long before supper parties and cool drinks at noon became a feature. There was of course a lot to gossip about but the most interesting gossip centred around Mrs L, a striking-looking woman of about forty-five, always beautifully groomed and turned out, courteous and also friendly. She had the best and most expensive cabin on the ship. Also onboard was a typical roué, a continental who had been in China for years. I do not think Mrs L and the roué had met before, but they certainly clicked. He became her constant companion for the rest of the voyage; they mixed well, went ashore together, and threw the most elaborate supper parties. We certainly enjoyed their company; in fact, one was upset if not on her invitation list. I had never met her before but in the back of my mind there was a niggling suspicion, confirmed one evening by a fellow passenger returning to Shanghai.

He informed me that Mrs L. was in fact the owner of one of the most expensive houses of ill fame in Bubbling Well Road, Shanghai. Those who knew kept mum, for they were great fun to be with; so it was the best kept secret east of Suez.

I was glad to see Hong Kong again – the hills, the harbour, the Hong Kong Club and the large business houses with their house flags flying. Now back to work and Hong Kong life.

In the early 1920s China was in turmoil. The Manchus had been overthrown and China's strong man Yuan Shi-kai was dead; there was in fact no central rule. The land was in the hands of the warlords.

The one outstanding person who set about trying to bring his country together and get rid of warlords and undue foreign influences was Sun Yat-sen. He was a patriot, republican, revolutionist and idealist who was to devote his life trying to unify his country and improve the lot of the poor. Sun Yat-sen who spent some of his time in Hong Kong was respected by all good people but sadly he died in 1925 long before his work was completed. His successor Chiang Kai-shek (Jiang

Jieshi) was very much less of an idealist and although he unified much of China he had immense problems in dealing with the warlords, the Chinese Communist Party and the expansionist policies of the Japanese. It was quite remarkable that business could prosper amongst such turmoil. But more of that later.

Connie was certainly an artist

Connie Berg, 1920s

*Connie and Sverre in
Norway, 1922*

CHAPTER 21

SUN YAT-SEN AND CHIANG KAI-SHEK

'Nationalism, Democracy, Equalisation' – Dr Sun Yat-sen

Chiang Kai-shek (standing) with Sun Yat-sen (New York Times)

I n 1643 the Chinese General Wu San-kue and his detachment of troops had the duty of guarding a strategic pass through the Great Wall of China on the Manchurian border.

While on duty General Wu received word that his beloved concubine in Peking had been carried off by the leader of a peasant army that had occupied the capital. Wu was broken-hearted and furious. He opened the gates in the wall and invited the Manchu army into China to help him find his concubine and destroy the peasant army.

The Manchus came and stayed for 267 years. They set up the Qing dynasty and conquered the whole country. Although accepted north of the Yangtze River, they were never liked in southern China. In spite of the fact that the Manchus adopted a number of Chinese customs as well as Confucian principles, nevertheless they remained distinct in a number of ways. Manchu women did not have bound feet; Manchu men wore pigtails and encouraged the Chinese to do so. Intermarriage between Chinese (the Han people) and Manchus was forbidden up till 1902, and finally and importantly, Manchus were given preference in official appointments.

When China was defeated by Japan in the first Sino-Japanese war (1895), European powers, having finished carving up Africa, set about carving up China and viciously competed for 'spheres of interest' in the middle kingdom (China).

The Imperial Court in Peking did not have the will or power to resist the foreign incursions. Instead it responded by giving aid and support to various societies with strong anti-foreign views. One of these societies, the Righteous Harmony Society, also had anti-Imperial views, but was enticed to drop its anti-Imperial stance and focus on attacking foreigners.

In rural northern China during the late nineteenth century there evolved two secret societies with strong anti-foreign sentiments, the Big Sword Society and the Spirit Boxers. Both were non-hierarchical organisations made up of young farmers, seasonal agricultural labourers and unemployed drifters. They practised various rituals, 'mass spirit possession', deep breathing exercises (qugong), martial arts and ritual boxing. They believed themselves to be impervious to bullets.

Both societies amalgamated to become the Righteous Harmony Society; to the westerners they were known as 'Boxers'. Their main aim was to oppose the land rights and privileges acquired by foreigners, in particular the missionaries in northern China, and to take back the land they owned and kill their Chinese converts. They adopted the slogan, 'Exalt the dynasty and destroy the foreigners.'

The first sign of unrest occurred in Shandong Province in 1898 in response to German and British encroachments. Missionaries were murdered and their property ransacked. This lead to overseas governments stationing small detachments of soldiers in their legations in Peking. This proved to be a wise precaution.

In 1900, tens of thousands of Boxers joined by elements of the Imperial Army attacked foreign compounds in Peking. Fortunately most foreign compounds and legations were located in close proximity to each other (except the German legation) and together they were able to defend themselves.

Under the overall command of the British minister to China, Claude Maxwell MacDonald, a small number of regular naval troops, utilising small arms fire and a single muzzle loading cannon, were able to hold off thousands of poorly armed Boxers and imperial troops for nearly two months, until relieved by an international force of over 50,000 men. Before this relieving force entered the city, Empress Ci Ki, disguised as a peasant, escaped in a cart and remained away from her capital for nearly a year.

While in power, the Boxers murdered foreign missionaries, their children and many thousands of Chinese Christians. This whole tragic episode was made worse by the atrocities and looting of Chinese treasures by elements of the relieving force.

In the end the Imperial Court was forced to sign the 'Boxer Protocol'. This entailed the execution of ten high ranking court officials and Boxers responsible for the murder of European missionaries and reparation in fine silver to the value of approximately £74 million sterling.

Anti-Manchu sentiment, in spite of the 'Boxer uprising' in northern China was mainly located in the south and with the weakening of central authority and the granting of foreign concessions during the nineteenth century, serious republican organisations began to appear in southern China. One such organisation the Revive China Society appeared during the 1890s. This society was organised by Sun Yat-sen (Sun Yixian), a patriot and idealist who is today recognised by Chinese of all political persuasions as the father of the revolution.

Sun Yat-sen was born in 1866 to a farming family in south east China not far from Hong Kong. His early schooling was traditional Chinese; then, at the age of thirteen, he joined his brother in Honolulu and entered a Church of England boarding school where he completed his secondary schooling. Sun then returned to Hong Kong, was baptised a Christian and enrolled in the newly founded Hong Kong College of Medicine, receiving much of his practical training at the Alice Ho Miu Ling Nethersole Hospital (founded by the London Missionary Society) and graduated with duel certificates in medicine and surgery.

Sun, however, had little real interest in medicine. He was at heart a Chinese patriot and a republican. With no army behind him, Sun, a pragmatist, was quite able to work with other rebels and felt quite at home within the conspiratorial world of Chinese secret societies and local warlords especially if he thought they could help him overthrow the Manchu government in Peking.

In 1895 Japan defeated China in a brief and humiliating war. Sensing the time was ripe for an uprising, Sun attempted a rebellion in south east China. This failed, Sun became a marked man and he fled abroad. But this rebellion marked the beginning of serious republican agitation in China, and while abroad, Sun developed a new ideology which he termed the 'Three Principles of the People – Nationalism, Democracy, Equalisation'.

1887

Chiang Kai-shek was born in 1887 into a family of middle class salt merchants in a small village near Ningpo. His father died when he was three, so he was brought up by his mother who in his words 'was the embodiment of Confucian virtues'.

The China Chaing was born into was a medieval place. In Canton a semi-human monster with huge feet was sighted in the river. This creature was said to be the cause of plague (cholera).

In Shanghai a criminal was sentenced to stand in a specially constructed cage suspended over the river without food or water until he died. Further south, a judge conjured up the ghost of the dead man as a witness in a murder trial.

Reference: Jonathan Fenby, *Generalissimo and the China He Lost,* (East Roseville, Simon & Schuster, 2002). Frank Walsh, *A History of Hong Kong* (London, Harper Collins, 1994).

In 1909, the conservative and reactionary dowager Empress Ci Xi died and her nephew the three-year-old Pi Yu ascended the throne further weakening the power and influence of the Manchus in Peking. To counter the rising tide of dissent and rebellion, the Manchus called in their best general Yuan Shi-kai. Yuan was partially successful in suppressing outbreaks but noting the extent of the republican movement and being an opportunist, Yuan offered them his tacit support.

In 1911, while Sun Yat-sen was still abroad, an uprising occurred in Wuchang and quickly spread. This was the first revolution and was successful. Sun immediately returned and was named Provisional President of the new Chinese republic but without an army and in the interest of national unity, he resigned in favour of Yuan Shi-kai, China's strong man, on the proviso that national elections would be held within two years (i.e. in 1913).

Sun Yat-sen, in preparation for the forthcoming elections, transformed his revolutionary organisation into a mainstream political party. The Kuomintang or KMT, one of the founding members, was the young and ambitious Chiang Kai-shek.

As promised, the elections were held in 1913 and the KMT won a majority of seats but not the presidency. The political strongman Yuan Shi-kai, with his old fashioned outlook, dozens of concubines and traditional ways, had no intention of giving up the presidency. He arranged the assassination of an influential member of the KMT, expelled all the supporters of the KMT from the newly formed parliament and entertained thoughts of establishing himself as emperor. Sun Yat-sen was again forced to flee abroad, this time to Japan.

While in exile in Japan, Sun Yat-sen married Soong Ching-ling in 1914 (she was in fact his second wife). Ching-ling was twenty-six years younger than her husband, had an American college degree and came from the wealthy, influential, Soong family, she was highly intelligent and a political radical.

For a time Yuan Shi-kai and his military backers controlled China, and Sun Yat-sen's republicans lacked the military strength to challenge him. Then in 1916 Yuan suddenly died of septicaemia.

If things had been bad under the Manchus and then under Yuan, they were about to become much, much worse with the disappearance of any semblance of central authority. China, including the capital Peking, now fell into the hands of warlords and bandits. Sun Yat-sen's republicans and the KMT now lost what little influence they ever had north of the Yangtze River. They retained some influence in the south, particularly around Canton.

Then on 4 May 1919, outside the gate of Heavenly Peace and without any prompting from Sun Yat-sen, thousands of students took to the streets of Peking to protest against the concessions that had been given to Japan at the Paris Peace Conference. Further protests occurred throughout China and amongst the protestors was a poorly paid teacher, Mao Zedong (Mao Tse-tung) a new Marxist.

Mao Zedong

Mao was born into a fairly well to do peasant family in the province of Hunan on 26 December 1893.

He had no interest in farming and little real interest in farmers, but being an enthusiastic reader and writer, he was able to obtain a number of teaching positions. As a teacher, Mao never performed with distinction.

In June 1920 Mao met Professor Chen Tu-hsiu, China's foremost Marxist, in Shanghai. Chen was in the midst of forming the Chinese Communist Party (CCP) with the encouragement and financial backing of Moscow. It would appear that Mao was not a founding member of the CCP as the Chinese official history claims, but he was certainly an enthusiastic supporter. The truth is that initially Mao felt that Sun Yat-sen's KMT had far more prospects than the CCP. Following the death of Sun Yat-sen and the rise of Chiang Kai-shek, Mao's allegiance swung away from the KMT. He became leader of the Chinese Communist Party and in 1949 he became Chairman Mao, the ruler of China, a land of nearly a billion people.

Sun Yat-sen had returned to China after Yuan's death and with his wife, oscillated between Shanghai and Canton, the cities that seemed to offer him the greatest support. In 1923 they settled in Canton and Sun Yat-sen assembled a viable republican government supported by local military figures and members of the old Kuomintang. Peking and much of the north remained in the hands of warlords who had not recognised his authority.

The executive branch of the KMT at this time was made up of idealists, republicans, socialists, opportunists and communists. In fact, Sun Yat-sen, Chiang Kai-shek and Mao Zedong were all members during the early 1920s.

To defeat the warlords and unite China, Sun Yat-sen sought help from abroad. He was largely ignored by the Western democracies but received enthusiastic support from Moscow and the newly formed Soviet Union who sent military and political advisers and even arranged a political marriage between the KMT and CCP. The Soviet Union went on to pledge support for China's national unification.

During this time Chiang Kai-shek, who distrusted the communists, realised correctly that the KMT needed military muscle, so he pushed for the establishment of a military academy at Whampoa, down river from Canton. This was approved by the KMT and in 1924 Chiang Kai-shek was appointed commanding officer of the academy. He set about ensuring that officer recruits came from well to do families and were likely to be loyal to him.

Sun, with strong southern support, political help from Russia and an army officered by men from the Whampoa Academy, made plans to expand his Canton base, break the hold of southern warlords and link up with sympathetic forces in north China and unify the country. Before he was ready to embark on this project he received an invitation from powerful northern militarists to meet them in Peking to discuss further reunification moves. Sadly, Sun was now ill and tired (probably anaemic). Nevertheless, with great determination, he undertook the journey by ship to north China. On arriving in Peking, he became so weak that he could barely walk. He had to be taken to his lodging in an ambulance. Doctors found he had an inoperable liver cancer; he died a few days later in March 1925. Sun's body was laid to rest at a temple on the outskirts of Peking, where thousands of people, rich and poor, came to pay homage.

Sun's wish to unify China was taken up by his protégé Chiang Kai-shek, who led his army north across the Yangtze to subjugate the northern warlords. This northern expedition was successful, but in 1927 Chiang, ever distrustful of the CCP precipitated a massacre of communists in Shanghai, expelled all left wing elements from the KMT, sent all Russian advisors home and because he did not control Peking, which was in the hands of a warlord, he established his own capital in Nanjing (Nanking). Chiang then increased his prestige enormously by marrying the younger sister of Sun Yat-sen's widow; an attractive American college graduate. Before he could do so, he had to placate her relatives by divorcing his first wife (which was an arranged match when he was still a boy), renouncing his concubines and converting to Christianity.

By 1928, Chiang had gained nominal control of China, his forces soon occupied Peking and he arranged for Sun Yat-sen's body to be moved to Chiang's new capital, Nanjing, where an immense mausoleum was built.

In spite of the more recent official Chinese (communist) history' Chiang Kai-shek's government achieved a great deal especially considering the situation in China at the time of Pi Yu's abdication and the continued incursion into his country by the Japanese.

Due to Chiang, the warlords had lost much of their power. Some of the more distasteful foreign privileges were moderated; prices were stabilised, banks made more accountable, drug trafficking tackled, railways and roads built and the new life movement introduced, stressing Confucian moral values and personal discipline.

Despite all these achievements Chiang still had to face immense problems. Though most of the urban areas were under his control, the countryside remained under the influence of the much weakened but still active warlords and bandits. However, of greater threat was the increasing influence of the Chinese Communist Party amongst the peasants and the expansionist policies of Japan.

Chiang Kai-shek was eventually forced to make an agreement (under duress) with the CCP. This agreement, quite incredibly, was brokered by Zhang Xueliang, the young warlord of Manchuria. Nevertheless, deep suspicions remained and the bulk of the subsequent fighting against the Japanese was still carried out by Chiang Kai-shek's forces.

The second Chinese civil war broke out after the defeat of Japan in 1945 and was eventually won by the communists in 1949. Chiang Kai-shek with his entourage moved to Taiwan (Formosa) and ruled there till he died in Taipei, aged eighty-seven, in 1975.

Mao Zedong at the age of fifty-six became Chairman of the Chinese Communist Party and the ruler of the whole Chinese mainland. He controlled over a billion people, overthrew an army of four million to achieve this and killed many more to keep it. He died in 1976.

Confucius

'The Chinese have perfected moral science and that is the first of science.' – Voltaire

A well-established religion existed in ancient China 1000BC. It held a belief in a supreme deity called Tian. This deity presided over the cosmos, subsidiary gods and spirits, and elaborate rights were developed for their worship.

During this so called 'pre-Confucian' era, rulers of the various kingdoms and states in China employed specialists in spiritual matters to advise them on the heavenly world, the gods and deceased ancestors.

Confucius (the name is the Latinised form of 'Kung-Fu-tzu' – meaning great master) is reputed to have lived from about 551BC to 479BC during a very unsettled time in China. The country was divided into a large number of independent states, family unity had broken down and there was much lawlessness. Confucius was very concerned about this state of affairs and after holding a number of government appointments he became a travelling teacher. He believed that many of China's problems had occurred because each person no longer kept his or her proper place in society.

Confucius taught that within the family the proper place for each person was for a son to obey and honour his father, a wife to obey and honour her husband and for a younger brother to honour his elder brother. In return, those who were honoured had a duty to behave well, to love and protect those that honoured them.

What applied in the family should also apply within the state. Soldiers should obey and honour their officers, who inturn should obey and honour their king, who held the highest position in society. He, the king, was 'the sun of heaven' and as such had a duty to carry out the 'mandate of heaven', which was to care for his people.

If the king did not behave himself and was evil, the people could revolt, because by his acts he had lost the 'mandate of heaven'.

Confucius did incorporate the religion of ancient China in his teachings. He believed in a supreme deity, but it did not concern him greatly for his main concern was to restore harmony in society. Confucius lived and died in comparative obscurity but his teachings attracted thousand of students, and after his death 'Confucianism' was made the state religion, embraced by millions and lasted for over 2000 years.

References: Lo Hui-Min, *The Story of China* (Singapore, Angus & Robertson, 1970).

Peter Bishop & Michael Darton, *The Encyclopaedia of World Faiths* (London and Sydney, McDonald Orbis, 1987).

Jonathon Fenby, *Generalissimo and the China He Lost* (East Roseville, Simon & Schuster, 2002).

Stephen G Haw, *The Traveller's History of China* (Gloucestershire, Windrush Press, 1995).

Derek Berg, *My Paper Trail* (Nambour, Derek Berg, 2005).

The result of a Japanese bombing raid on Shanghai.
It has since been said that the photographer placed the baby
on the railway to enhance the affect of the photo.

CHINA'S GENERALISSIMO

Chiang at the height of his power
(Time Life)

CHAPTER 22

Sailing and Rowing

During my early days in Hong Kong I was fortunate in that the then Norwegian consul, M Steckmest, had the use of a beautiful cutter *La Cigale*. She was supposed to be a small replica of *Britannia*, King George's famous yacht designed by GL Watson in 1893. *La Cigale* was built in Kowloon dock and was a very pleasant craft to sail with a very fair turn of speed. We did a lot of racing and cruising in her, but I am not so certain that she was a fair model of Britannia.

I was often lent yachts by owners who went on home leave, sometimes for six months or more, so although I did not for some time own my own craft, I was able to do a lot of sailing.

Eventually I acquired my own boat, the nine ton yawl *Irene* more or less straight stemmed and with no engine. *Irene* had seen better days, but in this venerable craft I ploughed quite a furrow through the cruising waters that were the joy and beauty of Hong Kong.

We yachtsmen were of course spoilt in Hong Kong. We all had a boat boy (who sometimes lived on the yacht) who not only cared for the boat but if needed, would act as a deckhand during races or long weekends. If the boat boy accompanied us overnight he would sleep quite comfortably in the forward cabin with the anchor chain, spare ropes and tackle. He provided his own food, which he cooked on the small primus stove.

Club races round the marks were generally sailed on Saturday afternoons. Ladies' races were on Mondays with the boat boy usually acting as forward hand. Wednesday afternoons were set aside for those who could take time off and it was surprising how well the Wednesday afternoon races were patronised.

Ocean races were my favourite. They generally started on Friday night or Saturday morning; the courses were around one or more of the outlying islands around Hong Kong, or to Macao. There was, however, one annual event that was dear to my heart – sailed usually in late November or early December between a team of four A-class boats (Dragon class) sailed by British crews against four similar boats sailed by Scandinavians.

Then there was rowing and here I must devote a few words about the 'Great Dane' as he was generally known and who became a lifelong friend. A good looking chap, about six foot two inches, with blue eyes and a zest for life, Holger Dreyer arrived in Hong Kong before me and was quite a well-known character when I met him. Very friendly, with a friendship that lasted till he died in Hong Kong after World War II. He was Danish, hence his nickname. He would participate in any sport, with success in some and always with great pleasure, finding love in outdoor life. Although a fine helmsman, rowing was perhaps dearest to his heart and he was indeed a fine oarsman.

There were two rowing clubs in Hong Kong: the Royal Hong Kong Yacht Club; and the Victoria Recreation Club. There were also good clubs in Canton with a boathouse at Shameen and clubs further afield at Shanghai and Tientsin with crews who sometimes travelled to Hong Kong to compete. These intercity rowing events were referred to as 'interports'.

My experience as far as rowing was concerned had been confined to paddling a dinghy or fishing in Norwegian summer months, I had never stepped into a racing shell and outriggers were unknown to me. Holger Dreyer changed all that; he got me interested in the refined torture of pushing a boat through water against another team of young husky stalwarts. I caught on and became quite a devotee. Hard work and good coaching eventually turned me into a reasonable oar and we met with a measure of success at regatta time.

Just before going on leave the Great Dane and I took out the Murdock Challenge Cup against strong teams from the Royal Hong Kong Yacht Club and the Canton Rowing Club. This notable victory stirred Holger into greater heights. He set his sights on the Canton fours, which he would stroke in two months' time at Canton against crews from Shanghai and Tientsin. This was shortly after I had returned from leave and meant plenty of training.

It was hard work after the idleness of home leave; it meant six o'clock at the boat shed for at least a mile and a half before breakfast and a good spurt in the afternoon before dinner. Hard work but I enjoyed it. Hong Kong weather is not always ideal for rowing and the water could get quite rough at times, but I always enjoyed the early morning workouts when the weather was fine, the crew pulled well and the boat caught the rhythm and ran smoothly.

Now for the Canton regatta. As was the custom, we took the 10 pm night steamer for Canton on Friday night, expected time of arrival at Shameen (Canton) 7 pm next morning.

We always enjoyed our short trips on these quaint old side-wheelers, the accommodation was more than adequate and consisted of old fashioned roomy cabins, generally for two with an ensuite and breakfast if requested. Shameen was an international treaty port, a small island in the Pearl River opposite the city of Canton.

Shameen had a number of fine oarsmen in those days. I still remember a Swiss who regularly won the single sculls and there were of course a number of ex-Oxford and Cambridge rowers making up the crews not only from Canton but also from Hong Kong and Shanghai.

Canton regattas were always enjoyable and on that Saturday there were races in all classes and a large contingent of supporters especially from Hong Kong who had come upriver for the occasion.

In our race we started well and gradually took the lead by half a length from the Royals with Canton half a boat length in third place, but when approaching the finishing line, disaster, Holger's outrig collapsed, he fell backwards onto my hands and lap, the oar handle smashed into his face, there was blood everywhere whilst his blade floundered about trying to capsize the boat and all the while the coxswain roaring his head off, 'Row, row, row you fools,' while the Royals were creeping up but we had just enough momentum to cross the line first.

Poor Holger's face was a mess. We got him to a doctor who stitched him up and informed us that there was no structural damage. That night Shameen let its hair down; the hospitality at the outpost was something to remember. By lights out, the Great Dane was out of pain and in great shape.

Irene, late 1920s

*Sverre and
the 'Great Dane'*

CHAPTER 23

BUSINESS AND CONSULAR DUTIES

The manager of our firm retired in 1920 and I was appointed to succeed him at a time when the post war shipping boom was subsiding. Our firm, which had been an all out shipping business, had over the last five years also developed a general import and export business.

Following the war, there was a shortage of ships and as a result freight rates reached limits beyond ship owner's expectations so that there was a scramble for new ships. Owners queued up at ship builders' offices with ready made contracts for the builders just to sign on the bottom line.

But as expected, this rush for new ships proved the old axiom 'what goes up, must come down.' There was soon an oversupply; freight rates, which had gone up with a bang, now came rapidly down.

We were probably not quite so badly off as some of our competitors. Our shipping in the Far East had over the years developed into a close relationship between client and ship owners, especially with Chinese merchants. This resulted in regular freighter services between eastern ports.

In those days the colony of Hong Kong could hardly be called an industrial city, but things were moving and in particular ship building and ship repairs were very well catered for. On the Kowloon side was the Hong Kong and Whampoo docks and on the Hong Kong side, The Taikoo Dock & Ship Builders. These shipyards employed a large workforce of Chinese plus a mix of European and Chinese engineers and foremen. They were indeed sophisticated undertakings well able to accept for construction large ocean going vessels.

Strikes, boycotts and other labour troubles had not been a problem during the early years of the twentieth century, particularly in the shipping industry, but problems were to occur in the not too distant future due to a number of factors.

Besides ship building and repairs there were a number of small factories producing all sorts of goods from torches to bicycles and it was amazing at times to watch John Chinaman at work, he worked hard either for himself or a boss.

During World War I there was a drastic reduction in Europe's capacity to export goods to China; this made it essential for China and Hong Kong to develop industries. Labour was of course readily available. From 1914 to 1922 the number of looms in textile factories in China increased from 4800 to 19,000 but sadly working conditions in many of these factories was appalling, twelve hours or more a day, seven days a week often utilising child labour. Labour contractors recruited from the countryside and labourers received a minimal wage, minimal shelter and little food. The fact that many of these factories were foreign owned (increasingly Japanese) added to friction between the proprietors and workers and a fertile field for nationalist and communist agitators.

So times change, the availability of abundant cheap labour

had led to abuses by some labour contractors and factory managers.

At the same time Sun Yat-sen had sought help from overseas to unify China. Russia complied and sent not only military advisers but also political advisers so that communist ideas soon spread amongst factory workers and peasants. As Canton was Sun Yat-sen's main centre of influence, worker's discontent was first manifested there and soon overflowed into nearby Hong Kong early in 1924.

Trouble in Hong Kong started with the usual hints and rumours of foreign capitalistic injustices to workers and evolved into an anti-foreign campaign. Where it all really started is difficult to say, but Canton Bolsheviks no doubt had the biggest hand in the trouble. Unions were never prominent in Hong Kong before 1923 but suddenly they appeared everywhere, their members making loud demonstrations and unrealistic demands leading to a general strike.

While all this was going on, we in Hong Kong had a most unpleasant time. Work came to a standstill, ships no longer discharged their cargoes, crews left, ships were not serviced and newspapers not printed. Every household lost its servants in spite of the fact that most domestic servants were not keen on leaving their jobs, which often included accommodation and food.

During the strike food was never a problem. Chinese storekeepers remained in business, but the previously pampered European housewives now had to do their own shopping, where previously it had all been done by their houseboys. They had also to look after their own children as their amahs were enticed to leave.

During this time the Hong Kong Club became the focal centre for the European community. The members operated the club quite satisfactorily. As newspapers were not printed, the club became the main source for information and everyday a government officer would appear at the club and disseminate the latest news.

Just prior to these difficult times I became Consul for

Norway and one of my first difficult tasks was to deal with a tricky problem in Canton. A Norwegian ship had been seized by supporters of the strike in Canton after discharging her inward cargo, which I was led to believe included guns and ammunition.

The Hav

Perhaps the Hav looked something like this? DB

One of Chiang Kai-shek's prime aims as leader of the military arm of the Kuomintang was to establish a military academy. The site chosen was an old military fort on Whampoo Island, ten miles downstream from the city of Canton.

Three days after the opening of the academy, the French community in Canton gave a dinner for the visiting governor of French Indo-China within the confines of the foreign concession on Shameen Island opposite the Canton bund (foreshore). As soup was being served a bomb was thrown through an open window into the dining room. Three of the diners were killed on the spot and two died later in hospital.

The Shameen authorities (being a treaty settlement Shameen was outside Chinese jurisdiction) immediately decreed that all Chinese had in future to show a photograph and pass to gain entrance to Shameen Island after dark. The Canton Government made up of republicans and members of Sun Yat-sen's Kuomintang immediately protested. Chinese workmen withdrew from the island and pickets isolated the concession from the city. Foreign women and children were evacuated to Hong Kong and all supplies to the island had to be shipped in from the colony.

In spite of compromises over Shameen, the tension increased; the radicalism of the Canton workers was encouraged by Russian advisers and left wing members of the KMT. Chinese businessmen became fearful of the aggressiveness of the 'red elements' in the city and to protect themselves they formed a khaki-clad militia named the Merchant Volunteer Corps or MVC, headed by a rich merchant and comprador for the Canton branch of the Hong Kong and Shanghai Bank, Chen Lien-po. Chen insisted that the MVC was nothing more than a self-defence force and needed guns and ammunition. Some suggested that Chen had an ally in Hong Kong, no other than the chief manager of the Hong Kong & Shanghai Bank.

To arm the men of the MVC it was decided to import a large quantity of small arms, 10,000 rifles and pistols together with several million rounds of ammunition. This was of course contrary to British policy and to all existing agreements with China. To ship the arms to Canton (probably from Hong Kong) a Norwegian freighter, The Hav was chartered. So a non-British, non-Chinese freighter steamed up the Pearl River with a consignment of arms for the MVC. This was in fact nothing more than a gun-running enterprise and possibly being carried out with the complicity of a senior member of a major and respected bank.

The plot was exposed and, on Sun Yat-sen's orders, the cargo of arms seized and the ship impounded. Deals were made, money changed hands, a compromise was reached and as a result half the arms were returned.

Subsequently fighting broke out between the MVC and Sun Yat-sen's republicans. The MVC were soundly defeated, their leader Chen Lien-po fled to Hong Kong and the British Communist Party sent a telegram to Sun Yat-sen: 'Hearty congratulations for your gallant struggle against foreign imperialism and native capitalism.' The remaining problem was the Norwegian ship the *Hav*. This problem was solved as usual with money and on this occasion by the intervention of the Norwegian consul from Hong Kong!

Fortunately the trains still ran, so I betook myself and travelled in my official capacity as Consul for Norway to Canton. I went to the strikers' headquarters and sat down with their leader who was indeed of the deepest red. After a long session I obtained an agreement, which certainly cost the ships owners' money (which the Chinese charterers agreed to repay). The crew turned up next morning and the ship steamed back to Hong Kong.

During these uncertain times there was one item the Hong Kong Government was very concerned about, the forthcoming visit to the colony by the Prince of Wales who would be arriving on the battle cruiser, HMS *Renown* towards the end of the year. All in Hong Kong were most anxious to entertain the prince and heir to the throne and to put on a 'good show'. Somehow or other the strike must be settled in good time.

How the strike was finally settled I am unable to say. Suddenly there were rumours, a government official went to West Point, the Hong Kong base for the striking unions, and suddenly it was all over. Union billboards disappeared and ships began to move again. The number one Hong Kong Club boy, named 'Tadpole', and his staff reappeared and commenced their duties ladling out the nectar to thirsty members.

There was more to it than that of course, there must have been some strings pulled, I expect some important Chinese had a hand in the settlement and no doubt money changed hands. Whatever the deal there were no fuss, no recriminations and no answers. Life almost instantly returned to normal to be quickly replaced by excitement engendered by the royal visit.

Decorative invitations were printed, designer gowns appeared, beauticians did a roaring trade and Hong Kong had a very major makeover. So that by the time HMS *Renown* entered harbour every important ship, person, regiment and officer was at his or her appointed place.

For the prince's arrival a public holiday was declared and Hong Kong put on a great party – bunting, red carpet and flags. The Chinese, who really know how to put on a party, performed their tiger and dragon display, Chinese music and everlasting fire crackers. Then the rounds of parties and receptions, dinners and balls, gaiety and amusements in the grand style, which I am pleased to say included members of the consular service and their ladies.

Finally a few decorations were distributed; two knighthoods went to Chinese and one or two to prominent Europeans. Yes, it may be truly said, the colony did the prince proud.

Sverre Berg with other members of the Hong Kong consular service

CHAPTER 24

SHIPS I KNEW

The author's impression of Dagmar asleep on Koh Phra Thong

In the autumn of 1914 the German steamer *Dagmar* left Hamburg for Bangkok with a cargo of steel rails and gunnies (sackings). She experienced an uneventful run out, the skipper's only anxiety being the worsening international situation and it is not difficult to visualise that as the voyage progressed he would be wondering if he would be able to avoid the ships of the Royal Navy and ever get to Bangkok!

By the time he reached the Gulf of Siam, war had been declared by Great Britain and France against his country and the prospect of his ship being captured as a prize was a real one. He was nearing the end of his voyage when he became aware of British warships in the vicinity. The skipper by looking at his charts noted that there were several small islands ahead, so he decided to run her ashore on one of these rather than see her taken by the enemy. She could, he reasoned, remain beached until the war was over and then reclaimed. So he ran her up on the beach of Koh Phra, the old quarantine station south of Bangkok. There she stayed for three years, sitting high and partly out of the water near the quarantine station.

In 1917 Siam (Thailand) joined the allied cause, so upsetting the skipper's plans. The Siamese authorities now declared *Dagmar* a prize. She was given to a high government official for services rendered. He was anxious to cash in on this valuable windfall and contracted our firm to arrange salvage and reconditioning. A contract was made out, a repair team despatched to commence repairs and I was directed to go to Koh Phra to be on the spot and assess the likely value of the salvage.

When I arrived the shipwrights had already started building the cofferdam over the midsection in readiness for pumping. I noticed that although she was partly aground, her after section was high out of the water. I was surprised at this as in Hong Kong we had been assured her cargo was intact; so I could not understand how she could have worked her way up shore with 2500 tons of rails in her plus gunnies and other odds and ends. I soon found there was not a rail left in her; they had all been stolen. As the cargo represented a valuable contribution to the salvage we had of course requested our Bangkok agents to obtain all information regarding the state of the cargo prior to my departure to Siam. They produced the manifests and we understood that the agent had appointed a surveyor to report on the cargo as well as on conditions in general. Their report was obviously inaccurate!

However, there wasn't much I could do about it now. Where the rails had gone was difficult to say, but knowing the waterfront and 'they that go down to the sea in ships' I had no illusions as to the possible fate of the rails. Not far from Koh Phra are the islands of Koh Shi Chang where ships of deep draft used to lighten before crossing the bar for Bangkok. There we found contractors with barges and cargo boats, as well as labour who would be glad to make a deal and steal the rails. So the cargo, had obviously been lifted out and sold on the black market whilst the ship remained on the beach at Koh Phra.

The ship herself seemed to be in reasonable condition and there were optimists who predicted she would be ready for sea again in a month's time. But it took six months to recondition her. We had to tow her to Hong Kong as we found Bangkok was not equipped for the amount of work required. Fortunately her machinery and boilers were better than anticipated but the shell plating was badly pitted where she had rested on her starboard side, and part of this had to be renewed.

The tow to Hong Kong was a bit of a risk; the typhoon season was on but we decided this was a gamble worth taking as one generally gets fine weather between typhoons, and of course there are a couple of good anchorages on the way up. Fortunately all went well.

By the time she arrived in Hong Kong she flew the British flag and her name had been changed to *Hoi Mah*, Chinese for seahorse.

She immediately went into dry dock and once again became a good looking ship. We gave her quite a launching to speed her on her new life. Her Siamese owner was very proud of her, even when the bills were totted up.

We started her on the rice run with cargoes from Bangkok and Saigon to Hong Kong and Shanghai. She did very well and became quite a favourite with charterers and skippers, her officers stayed with her and so did her Chinese crew; she was earning money and her costly repairs were gradually paid off.

This continued for about two and a half years when an offer of purchase was made to her owner by a syndicate in Shanghai. It was a fair offer; it would pay off all debts and leave a bit over for the owner. 'Manna from heaven,' he called it.

The buyers were northern Chinese and when it came to handing over the purchase money they produced three suitcases, with a collection of strange notes of various denominations, all originating from North China. When our comprador saw this weird collection of bank notes he immediately described it as 'bandit loot' and that obviously was what it was. The civil war was on and a number of so-called warlords were looting the country and the people, setting up their own governments, printing their own bank notes and generally devastating everything like a swarm of locusts.

Their money was of course unacceptable to us but they were most insistent on buying and requested time to have their spurious money converted. The owner was keen to sell, we gave them four days, never expecting they would come back, but they did. They must have had some close connections with Chinese banks and they paid up in good Hong Kong currency.

We discharged our officers and crew as the new owners had their own men ready to take over. The transfer took only a couple of days and I suddenly found myself saying goodbye to the ship I had wakened from her sleep on the beach at Koh Phra and become quite attached to.

She had proved herself an acquisition, a well mannered little vessel that had made a niche for herself. Now she was leaving us and I thought she looked rather despondent with the Chinese flag hanging over her stern as she made her way slowly through Lye Moon pass.

They were to call at Amoy where they stayed four days. There they took on board some 600 soldiers from the local warlord.

There was no further news until a rumour reached me a few days later, to the effect she had gone aground on the saddles, the well-known mark for Woo Sung and became a total wreck.

I gradually got the story from one of the Shanghai pilots who had discussed it with the mate of *Hoi Mah*.

Well, it was a dark night but the weather was reasonable, a

good deal of flood was coming down the river (Yangtze) but we were on our bearing for the entrance and had no doubt about our position. We felt the ship lift a couple of times but assumed this was caused by the flood water. Then she suddenly took matters into her own hands and took a hitch towards the rocks and struck, not hard at first, but then she made sure by lifting again and sort of wrapped herself round the island – that was it.

Believe me, ships have souls and great pride. I have no doubt that *Hoi Mah* had no intentions of becoming involved in China's civil war by carrying soldiers for northern warlords, so sadly she took matters into her own hands and committed suicide on the saddles.

During the late 1920s there were four river steamers that ran out of Hong Kong. Two of them for the Canton run and two for the Macao service. The *Sui An*, the matriarch was a paddle steamer built in 1899, and the *Leungshan*, a little younger, was built in 1923. The other two, the *Fatshan* and *Kinshan*, were of slightly more recent vintage.

They were all quite comfortable old ladies and filled the need as conventional links with the two outports. They had also served their shareholders well, but with the opening of the Hong Kong to Canton railway, the river traffic to Canton was showing signs of tapering off; the business was not what it used to be, so the owners had decided to dispose of them.

Friends of mine in Shanghai were interested and made an offer for *Sui An* and *Leungshan*, which led to lengthy negotiations. Both parties being Chinese, it was difficult to arrive at a suitable price; however, eventually the deal went through.

These vessels had become very popular and had for years been part and parcel of the Hong Kong harbour scene and quite a sentimental attachment had grown up around them. They had in fact become one of the recognised landmarks of Hong Kong. The newspapers printed their history and wrote of the wonderful service they had been to the colony. Especially *Sui An* with her ponderous side wheels stomping along with her compound engine, churning up quite a gusher with every spoke of the wheel.

When the time came for their departure, quite a number of shipping and commercial people gathered on the bund to see them off and wish them good speed and luck. The ships were dressed in all their bunting; I think the skipper of *Sui An*, who was to lead, was just about to blow the hooter when a Chinese brass band appeared and rendered *The Washington Post*. Their repertoire was not very extensive, so they gave us a couple of repeats and finished up with variations from *The Merry Widow*. It was all very festive and then became solemn; and I who had started the ball rolling became a bit apprehensive and wondered if I would find myself thrown into the harbour. However, all went well and they finally got away with *Sui An* leading.

My version of Sui An

They both called at Swatow and Amoy to show the flag. I am glad to say they had a reasonable voyage and duly arrived at Woo Sung where they tied up and began their new life on the Yangtze.

The other two, *Fatshan* and *Kinshan* continued their run between Hong Kong and Macao. They were still giving good service when *Kinshan* was chartered by the Royal Navy and went on active service in the Gulf of Bengal; her shallow draft made her particularly useful for patrolling along the shores of Burma and India.

I next met *Kinshan* when returning from a business trip to Bangkok on the cargo steamer *Diva*, one of our agency vessels. It was on a bright sunny morning when we sighted *Kinshan*, who hailed us just off the Vietnam coast, requesting us to come alongside. She was flying the naval ensign and signalled us by flag hoist. It appeared that she was out of food, fresh water and her fuel was running short. She was on her way back to Hong Kong; they had obviously been on petrol for some time. We had a full cargo of rice, plenty of groceries, plenty of fresh water and fuel to spare, the difficulty being to transfer all of this across from ship to ship.

Captain Jorgensen suggested we go into Cam Ranh Bay (Vietnam, then French Indo China) to sort things out and this we did. Cam Ranh Bay was just under our lee, a beautiful place with green clad hills, perfect unblemished nature that had not yet been ravaged by humans, as the place unfortunately became later.

Diva anchored and *Kinshan* came alongside, after which the transfer of goods went smoothly. We supplied them with sufficient stores to reach their destination so they had an untroubled voyage to Hong Kong. I subsequently met the captain of *Kinshan* in Hong Kong and we settled the accounts for the goods; he was of course very thankful for the service rendered, but *Kinshan* looked rather dilapidated, which was not surprising as she had had little or no maintenance for some time. So we arranged for *Kinshan* to go into dock for a complete make-over so she could return with dignity to her old run.

It was during this trip that I became shipmates with live pigs, the 'black saddle backed' variety, the real Chinese breed.

During our completion of loading in Bangkok the captain was told that on his way up to Hong Kong he was to call at Hainan to pick up a cargo of live pigs, 1200 of them, for Hong Kong. I should perhaps mention that this was quite a common cargo to carry on that run, but was generally reserved for Chinese coastal vessels. The distance is only some 125 miles from Hainan to Hong Kong, just an overnight run. The *Diva* was a small vessel of some 2000 tons only and I was wondering how they would find room for so many animals. But that was easily done; each pig was enclosed in an open straw basket rather like a cocoon, and in these they were stowed in orderly rows to enable the coolies looking after them to pass in between to give them fresh water. However, they got no food during the passage; the skipper did not want their bowels to function!

The ship's personnel did not like these cargoes; livestock is different to the ordinary commodities they carry. Only the gold-toothed cook smiled – probably saw the prospect of scrounging a porker or two from the tally.

The weather was fine – beautiful holiday weather with clear skies, nice warm sun but no wind. 'Oh what price for a nice breeze,' the mate groaned, 'but as usual, nary a bloody breath of air when we most need it to disperse the smell generated by 1200 pigs.'

The porkers certainly hummed, all the way to Hong Kong; and the flies came too, all sorts of them by the thousands: bush flies (the nippy ones that give you no peace), horse flies, blow flies; even house flies; but the most obscene ones were the fat shiny ones, all the time gorging on what the pigs left behind. I could not help pitying the poor swine. The ship certainly was no garden of roses with that lot on board.

Still there are individuals amongst the pork society, adventurous ones who forever strove for something better. There was one squealing to high heaven having lost its tail, the neighbour to the rear had been able to get its snout sufficiently through the rattan to reach the others rear and happily munched the titbit, while the owner proclaimed the loss to the wide. When the coolies came round in the afternoon to give the pigs water, they raised a hullabaloo, which 1200 hungry, full-grown pigs are capable of producing, and were probably heard for miles; but as the skipper had ordered, all they got was fresh water. 'Fill them up to the gills,' he said, 'to make them put on weight.'

The ship became strangely quiet after they were unloaded and gone, except for the sound of the ship's crew hosing the decks. When I reached home my wife had gone shopping, and Ah Mow, the house boy, gave me the day's news. 'And tonight Mr and Missi Fo'bes come for dinner. Cook making sucking pig and lice, velly nice!'

There was another ship I became quite attached to, if for no other reason than the fact that she was, to me, Jimmy Bullock's ship.

I had of course heard from Jimmy from time to time and when on leave had had meaningful discussions with Jimmy and his two uncles, who were the principle directors of the shipping company, Whitley Steam Navigation Company, the owners of the ill-fated *Gladiator* that had been torpedoed off southern England in 1917. They were planning to replace *Gladiator* with a new vessel and were interested in utilising her in the Far East and hoped that I would be involved in arranging charters and cargo for her.

Jimmy arrived from England with his new ship, *Gladiator II*, early in the new year. She was a fine ship, 4310 tons dead weight with a speed of twelve knots, a single screw coal burner as was usual in those days. They had a good trip out, a profitable one with a cargo of prefabricated steel from Newcastle to Rangoon, then a full cargo of rice from Rangoon to Hong Kong. Shortly after arrival, Jimmy, as arranged, repatriated his deck crew to England and replaced them with Chinese crew but retained his officers.

He informed me that Terese and the boys are well and that they will be visiting us later in the year. The boys go to school in England and spend their holidays in Nantes with the Lefevres.

As Jimmy is new to the Far East I took some time out to show him the ropes. I did a short trip with him to Swatow, introduced him to Chinese businessmen and in particular the comprador and his staff. Naturally it is important that the ship and its personnel earn a reputation.

We arranged to fit her out well, complete new awnings, plenty of fresh water and toilets (Asiatic of course), so that she could comfortably take 1200 deck passengers per voyage as well as cargo. In truth *Gladiator II* was very well suited for the China coast run and a welcome addition to our business. She was to spend many profitable years in the Far East and a spin off benefit was to see Terese again and spend happy times with Jimmy.

CHAPTER 25

SHANGHAI

Shanghai

Foreign Concessions

When the Treaty of Nanking was negotiated in 1842 (at the conclusion of the so-called Opium War) the British demanded a small plot of ground at Shanghai where they could build a trading station. Shanghai is not of course on the banks of the broad Yangtze River but ten miles from its mouth on the banks of the muddy Whangpoo tributary.

The Chinese picked out a spot that was of least value to them in the hope that the foreigners would soon get fed up, lose heart and go away. The site they offered was a mosquito-infested mud flat subject to flooding at every high tide.

The British nevertheless accepted the allotment, so the French also demanded one, as did the Americans. The three plots of land were of equal size, about two square miles each. Eventually the Americans and British amalgamated to form the International Settlement; the French decided not to join them and maintained their own French concession. These concessions were to remain in existence until the Japanese takeover during World War II.

Reference: Carl Crowe, *Foreign Devils in a Flowery Kingdom* (London, Hamish Hamilton, 1941).

B usiness made it necessary for me to visit Shanghai in order to conclude negotiations for the purchase of two coastal vessels with the New Engineering and Shipbuilding Company. The ships were nearing completion and I was interested to see the quality of their work. I must say I was pleasantly surprised on that score; but, as usual, completion was delayed for various reasons, the principal being lack of materials, which in China in those days indicated a shortage of capital! However, we came to an arrangement and the ships were to be handed over to us in three months time.

The shipbuilding yard and company was a recent undertaking, having been in existence for only four years; that is indeed young for a shipyard, whose breed generally runs into generations. It was in every respect a Chinese concern and I was interested to note that all the engineers had first class certificates, all had gone to a university and all had trained in foreign shipyards. I felt confident that they would turn out two good ships.

Shanghai is very different to Hong Kong. Hong Kong was of course a British colony where the leading banks and institutions were patterned on the customs and traditions of John Bull. Hong Kong in those days was more important commercially, catering for a large proportion of the Far East shipping trade. Shanghai on the other hand was a huge Chinese city containing within its boundaries two foreign concessions peopled by British, French, Americans, Filipinos, Jews and a large number of stateless White Russians. Amongst them were adventurers, revolutionaries, beggars, paupers, businessmen, millionaires and gangsters associated with widespread corruption. Nevertheless, during the 1920s and 1930s, Shanghai was an exciting place and far less staid than Hong Kong.

The Park

'Dogs and Chinese not allowed'

One day following the establishment of the International Settlement a small Chinese junk sunk in the muddy foreshore at the junction of the Whangpoo River and Soochow Creek. Silt built up around the wreck and added to the foreshore area. The English citizens suggested constructing an embankment, filling in the land and laying out a garden. A Scottish gardener was brought out from 'home', trees and shrubs imported and a small English type garden or park established.

The park became the centre of communal life for the Shanghai foreigners. Dogs were excluded and so were Chinese except for Chinese servants accompanied by their foreign employees, particularly amahs; but the sign 'dogs and Chinese not allowed' never existed. It was the stuff of gossip and later propaganda.

The park existed for many years before it occurred to many Chinese that they should be admitted unaccompanied. The authorities (Shanghai Municipal Council) felt that owing to the small size of the garden it would obviously be impossible to throw it open to the general public, but an attempt was made to meet Chinese desires by issuing a police order to the effect that the garden would be open to any well dressed native. The chance of being humiliated by a refusal was so great that few Chinese asked for admission.

Reference: Carl Crowe, *Foreign Devils in a Flowery Kingdom* (London, Hamish Hamilton, 1941).

After concluding our business, the director of the building yard decided I should join him at a 'Yam Singh' party before returning south. 'Yam Singh' in Cantonese means 'bottoms up'.

The evening started at Bubbling Well Road with a few drinks before moving to a rather upmarket Chinese restaurant where to my surprise we sat down with a number of attractive Chinese starlets, their cheongsams slit right up to their thighs. After the meal we moved over to the *Sun Flower Heaven* where we joined in the dancing on a sprung floor to an excellent band. Chinese and Europeans crowded the bars, men competing for women, women competing for men and all being offered exotic cocktails. Later some drifted upstairs where two roulette tables were in full swing; bets came fast and furious with free drinks served by gorgeous bar girls. Gambling is in every Chinaman's makeup and I suppose it will always be so, whether in business or in fun. But one could only be amused by the fact that gambling of all kinds was strictly prohibited in the confines of the International Settlement, but then corruption, extortion, prostitution and even murder were common in Shanghai in those days.

Later we were joined by Russian princesses from the *Cabaret Russe* and a little later by taxi girls from the less upmarket *Green Bottle* from across the road. They were all sisters under the skin getting what they can out of life in what was then a very uncertain time.

To round off the evening we had to pay a visit to *The Trenches*, a row of dance halls, a little more downmarket, where the taxi girls were cheaper and drinks suspect, but the gaiety and fun was no less hectic and the girls very attractive and persistent. But I was now feeling a bit woozy; it was time to find a rickshaw and return to my hotel while I could still think rationally.

The next day with a mild headache I was taken to what was then claimed to be the longest bar in the world. This claim had to be challenged and not surprisingly it was, by a number of Americans who told all and sundry that there was a longer bar in the United States.

Whatever the truth of the matter, the long bar in the Shanghai Club was truly a whopper. To see this in action on a Saturday morning with row upon row of men, four deep, being served by bar boys passing drinks over heads, across and around men's backs while everyone is talking and shouting. It was certainly a unique experience.

But all good things come to an end. That evening I boarded my steamer for Hong Kong. I had a very early night and vowed not to have a drink for a week. Shanghai was certainly a lot different to Hong Kong.

CHAPTER 26

FAMILY AFFAIRS

Bergslein, Stubbs Road, Hong Kong, 1930

I had for some time been considering severing my connection with my present company. I had now been a long time in somebody else's employ and I thought I should start being my own master. I had been fifteen years abroad and served a long apprenticeship, so I felt able to run my own show.

Perhaps the present was not the very best time to branch out, conditions were a little slack; but I told myself they might get better and I wanted to be there when conditions improved. So, at the end of November 1928, I took the fatal step. Looking back I can only say it was a courageous decision; there were to be bad times during the depression, but there were also some great years, and on balance I believe it was the right decision.

During the early 20s Connie and I had purchased a rather lovely house on Stubbs Road, two-thirds of the way up the peak with a beautiful view of Hong Kong; we named the house *Bergslein*. Connie loved it. Our son Derek was born on the 13 November 1926 and Connie was confined at the Matilda Hospital; all went well. Derek, like nearly all European children in Hong Kong, was immediately adopted by the servants and in particular by his amah Ah Chok. Early in 1929 Connie took Derek to Adelaide to show him off to his grandparents; it proved to be a very successful trip.

Sadly, shortly after their return, tragedy struck. Our second child, a little girl was stillborn and shortly after, Connie became very ill with cerebral malaria. She died on 20 October 1929. It was terrible.

I now had a little son without a mother – what to do? It so happened that friends from Adelaide were returning by ship to Australia from a cruise to Japan. They kindly offered to take Derek with his amah to Adelaide so that he could be cared for by his grandparents and aunts.

Being a bachelor again I became very much involved in business, sailing and the Royal Hong Kong Yacht Club. Holger Dreyer kept me rowing, which was a great help.

In 1932 I met and married Tui O'Kane, another attractive Australian girl from Sydney. Tui was doing a tour of the Far East. She had just graduated, following four years of nurse training at Royal Prince Alfred Hospital in Sydney. The tour was a gift from her mother. Tui and I were to live through some very difficult times, including the Depression and four years as prisoners of war, but it was a lovely marriage. We were to have a daughter Margaret Ann who was to be a great joy to us.

Shortly after our marriage, Tui returned to Australia to pick up Derek from his grandparents. She returned not only with Derek but with a kangaroo – quite a novelty in Hong Kong.

It was at that time that the world Depression hit Hong Kong. We had to sell *Bergslein*, discharge the servants, and no more yachting. We initially rented a flat and then moved to a much more humble abode near the Catholic cathedral and Tui went to work as a nursing sister to help keep the wolf from the door.

Unfortunately Tui while at work began to experience severe and incapacitating pain in her left arm. This proved to be due to a cervical rib (an extra rib at the base of her neck), which would have to be removed, meaning a delicate and unusual operation at that time.

With financial help from Tui's mother, it was decided she and Derek would again travel to Sydney for her operation and that Derek would remain in Australia under the care of his step-grandmother and step-uncle who had a sheep property near Inverell in NSW. Derek was to board at a private home with two other boys in Inverell so that he could go to the local school. We had visions that one day Derek would grow up in Australia and 'go on the land'.

Tui's operation was a success and she was soon back in Hong Kong where thankfully business began to improve. But our troubles were by no means over. Derek became very ill and it was some time before the problem was diagnosed. Eventually he had to be taken by his step-grandmother by train to Sydney from Inverell where a very large kidney abscess was drained. He recovered well and Tui and I felt it best for him to be brought back to Hong Kong. So off Tui went again to collect him. He soon settled down in Hong Kong and a year later we sent him to St Giles British School in Tsingtao, North China, to complete his primary school education.

As business improved during 1937/38 I felt I could now fulfil a long-held dream and have built my ideal yacht. She was, as was the custom in those days to be built of timber, forty feet from stem to stern, a lovely double-ended cutter. We named her *Marander* after my two children Margaret Ann and Derek. Sadly, I had her for only three years; she was destroyed when the Japanese took Hong Kong.

As war clouds gathered in Europe and China, we felt it wise to send our children to Australia to complete their schooling. Derek after three years at Tsingtao went to the Armidale School and a year later Margaret Ann went off to the New England Girls' School. Both schools were located in the same country town in New South Wales called Armidale. Although it meant boarding school for both children a long way from home, it proved to be a very wise move when later the Japanese army occupied Hong Kong.

Reference: Derek Berg, *My Paper Trail* (Nambour, Derek Berg, 2005).

Margaret Ann launches Marander

Marander, 1939

The Royal Hong Kong Yacht Club, late 1930s

Tui

Derek in Hong Kong

Margaret Ann

CHAPTER 27

THE WARLORD

Zhang Zuolin , the 'Mukden Tiger', later the 'Old Marshall'
(Generalissimo and the China He Lost, Jonathan Fenby,
Simon & Schuster)

D uring the 1920s and 1930s while the great colonial powers were preoccupied with Mussolini, Edward VIII, communism, Hitler and the Spanish civil war, momentous events were unfolding in China.

Following the fall of the Qing dynasty (Manchus), the country was ruled for a short period by Yuan Shi-kai, a virtual dictator and would-be emperor. He unexpectedly died in 1916. Following his death, central rule broke down in China completely and the country fell into the hands of a multitude of warlords. Civil war broke out and finally Japan invaded the country. Tends of millions were involved; millions died and horrible atrocities were committed.

The fifty years from 1890 to 1940 were the years of the Chinese warlords; often depicted in the West as comic opera generals with ostrich-plumed headgear, ornate uniforms bedecked with medals and braded epaulettes, but they were, in truth, cunning clever exponents of brute force. They went by various colourful names, the 'dogmeat general' (Zhang Zongchang) of Shandong province, the poetry writing 'philosopher general' (Wu Peifu) and the 'model general' of Shanxi province.

Some of these warlords controlled huge areas of China, printed their own money, established banks with no assets, taxed the farmers and appropriated their live stock to feed their soldiers. Murder, looting, kidnapping and extortion were common sources of income. Rich families were encouraged to pay large ransoms by being sent a severed finger or ear of a kidnapped love one!

To me the two most effective, sophisticated and influential warlords were Zhang Zuolin – also spelt 'Chang Tso-lin' – (the Old Marshall) and his son Zhang Xuelang (the Young Marshall) of Manchuria.

Manchuria is a vast land, the size of Germany and France combined. It is rich in minerals, coal, timber, agricultural products and furs. Part of the Chinese Empire under the Manchus, it was coveted by both Russia and Japan.

There was, however, a third player for control of Manchuria, Zhang Zuolin; short in stature, he first became a bandit and in his own words then graduated as a warlord at the 'University of the Green Forest'.

During the Russian–Japanese war (1904–1905) Zhang Zuolin sided with the Japanese, simply because they offered him more than the Russians. When the Japanese won, Zhang, ended up with arguably the largest army in China and, with his fast-charging cavalry, became a constant threat to Chinese rulers south of the Great Wall.

Manchuria, recognised by the great powers and later by the League of Nations as part of China, was in the early part of the twentieth century under the virtual control of Zhang Zuolin, now dubbed the 'Old Marshall'. He set up his capital in Mukden (She-nyang). He wisely recognised that southern Manchuria was under the influence of Japanese business interests and that in the north the Eastern Chinese Railway was administered by Russians based at Harbin. He dealt with both.

Following the first Chinese revolution and the fall of the Manchus (1911) China's strong man and effective ruler Yuan Shi-kai in Peking ordained the Old Marshall Governor of Manchuria (he had little choice); but when Yuan Shi-kai attempted to mount the Peacock throne and proclaim himself Emperor of China, the Old Marshall, and now the governor of Manchuria, said 'No' and Yuan failed. The issue was finally resolved when Yuan died in 1916.

By 1920 Zhang was extending his influence south into China proper and in 1924 he pushed beyond the Great Wall and occupied Peking. He next set up a government of North China and Manchuria, which was even recognised by a number of the great powers but not by the League of Nations. Nevertheless, he now ruled an area the size of Western Europe.

The Old Marshall was now at the height of his power. He took to wearing elaborate uniforms, including a skull cap with the largest pearl in the orient over his forehead. He had, however, a number of problems: the first, a flamboyant but clever, fun-loving son who experimented with drugs and led an unstable and seemingly irresponsible lifestyle. The second problem was much more sinister: the Japanese, who had now stationed an army (the Kwantung army) in southern Manchuria ostensibly to protect Japanese business interests and the southern Manchurian railway. The third problem was Chiang-Kai-shek and his nationalist army, which was advancing on Peking from the south in an endeavour to eliminate all warlords and unite China.

'One Arm Sutton'

Francis Arthur Sutton was born in England in 1884. Educated at Eton, he grew up to become a talented engineer with an obsession for golf. In his early twenties he was employed developing railways in Argentine and Mexico.

At the outbreak of World War I he immediately joined the British Army, was commissioned and sent to Gallipoli. He arranged to take his golf clubs with him. Sadly he lost his right arm in combat and was from then known as 'One Arm Sutton'. However, he continued to play golf and remained serving with the troops at Gallipoli and he became quite a legend.

Following the war 'One Arm' went prospecting for gold in Eastern Siberia, where he came to the notice of the Manchurian warlord Zhang Zuolin, the Old Marshall. Zhang recruited 'One Arm' into his own private army as his advisor with the rank of General.

The story goes that 'One Arm' taught the old warlord how to play poker. He did not teach him well but Zhang became addicted to the game, he would sit down with half a dozen of his generals, including 'One Arm' and play till the early hours of the morning. At the end of each poker session, the Old Marshall, who was invariably the big loser, simply handed out IOU chits for fabulous sums of money to the winning generals, who politely accepted them in lieu of cash. None except 'One Arm' would dare make a claim on Zhang's IOU chits.

It was said that 'One Arm' would always claim on the Old Marshall's chits and was always promptly paid in full. This resourceful soldier of fortune went one step further. He bought the other winning general's chits for half price and then claimed and obtained their full value from the Old Marshall.

In 1928 Zhang Zuolin was killed, forcing 'One Arm' to find other patrons. He went on to make and lose fortunes in both China and Canada. He was well able to deal with Chinese warlords, Japanese generals and Russian diplomats during those turbulent years prior to World War II; but in the end, the Japanese had had enough of 'One Arm'. He was captured during World War II and imprisoned in Hong Kong, where he sadly died in 1944.

Reference: Ronald Farquharson, *Confessions of a China Hand,* (London, *Hodder & Stoughton, 1950).*

Facing a two-pronged attack by Chiang Kai-shek's army to reclaim China's old capital (Peking), the Old Marshall felt it prudent to leave Peking and return to his capital, Mukden, well north of the wall and in Manchuria.

On 3 June 1928, twenty cars drove up to the Peking railway station. Zhang smilingly entered his private cobalt blue carriage while a military band played a lively tune. The train started its journey north.

The next day, 4 June, the Old Marshall sat smoking a cigar while his train entered the outskirts of Mukden, now Shenyang. As his carriage passed under a bridge an explosion brought down a span, which fell onto his carriage. Still alive, Zhang was helped from the train by a Japanese advisor, but Zhang was badly injured and bleeding heavily from his nose and face. It took twenty minutes for a car to arrive, which drove him to his residence. He then started to vomit blood, so they transferred him to a Japanese hospital; four hours later the Old Marshall was dead.

The assassination was the work of officers attached to the Japanese Kwantung army, almost a law unto themselves. They saw the Old Marshall as an obstacle to their expansionist schemes and fully expected more cooperation from his son and successor, the playboy Zhang Xuelang; they were in for a rude shock.

After his father's funeral, Zhang Xuelang was told brutally that Tokyo was determined to prevent any agreement between Manchuria and the Chinese government of Chiang Kai-shek. However, there was much more to Zhang Xuelang, now dubbed the 'Young Marshall', than either the Japanese or even the Chinese anticipated. He reminded the Japanese that he, the son of a warlord, the former governor of Manchuria, was Chinese; and to emphasise this point he later had two pro-Tokyo officials executed in front of all his guests at one of his dinner parties! Nevertheless, by skilled diplomacy, he continued to encourage the Japanese to invest in Manchuria, while at the same time making friends with Chiang Kai-shek and his talented wife Madam Chang Kai-shek. In return, Chiang Kai-shek, now virtual ruler of China, appointed Zhang Xuelang to succeed his father as governor of Manchuria.

In 1932 the Japanese Kwantung army, using the excuse that Chinese soldiers had sabotaged a section of the railway track outside Mukden, took over Manchuria. Both Chiang Kai-shek and Zhang's private army did not have the fire power to prevent the Japanese takeover. This act was taken without authority from Tokyo and in spite of appeals to the League of Nations by Chiang Kai-shek.

Although the Japanese government had not authorised the takeover they now accepted it as a 'fait accompli' they renamed Manchuria, Manchukuo and installed the deposed emperor of China, the twenty-eight-year old Pi Yu as emperor, Kang Teh of Manchukuo and installed him in a replica of Peking's Temple of Heaven (after all he was a Manchu). To complete the takeover, Japan resigned from the League of Nations (the first nation to do so), which was to them becoming more and more ineffectual.

Following the Japanese takeover Zhang Xuelang moved south of the border with his Manchurian army and joined Chiang Kai-shek in his efforts to overcome the remaining warlords and Mao's communist army, south of the Yangtze River. This campaign south of the river was successful as far as overcoming the warlords; but the communist army, although surrounded, managed to escape through that section of Chang's army manned by unreliable irregulars. Mao's communists then embarked upon the now famed long march west and then north to Yeuans province in north China.

During the late 1920s and 1930 Chiang Kai-shek persisted in utilising most of his forces to eliminate the Chinese red army instead of tackling the Japanese army and ejecting them from Chinese territory, including Manchuria.

The Young Marshall, although basically loyal to Chiang Kai-shek, began to have doubts about Chiang's policy, which entailed Chinese fighting Chinese instead of combining to fight the Japanese, who after all had killed his father and stolen 'his' country.

Having noted the widespread support for the Chinese Communist Party amongst the Chinese peasants, Zhang made contact with Chou En-lai, Mao's second in command. The Young Marshall was convinced that Chiang Kai-shek could not suppress communism in China and on 6 April 1936 Zhang had a meeting with Chou En-lai, without the knowledge of Chiang Kai-shek. Both men agreed that a united front against Japan was essential.

Later that year Chiang Kai-shek having overcome problems in the south planned another campaign against the communists north of the Yangtze. He moved north with his army and established his headquarters at Xi'an (Si'an), capital of Shanxi province, just south of the remnants of the communist army.

Early in the morning of 12 December 1936 Chiang Kai-shek while asleep was kidnapped by Colonel Sun and a 120-strong detachment of troops loyal to Zhang and taken to the 34-year-old Young Marshall who had engineered the whole plot.

Over the next few weeks, Madam Chiang Kai-shek and Chou En-lai were flown into Xi'an and an agreement hammered out between communist and nationalist to unite under the overall command of Chiang Kai-shek with the express purpose of fighting the Japanese.

Xi'an

Qin Shihuang, China's first emperor: perhaps he looked like this?

Along the fertile Wei River (a tributary of the Yellow River) valley over a period of 2000 years a number of cities evolved, all in such close proximity to each other that in some cases they merged. They went under different names, the most significant of which were Changan (Ch'angan) and Xi'an (Si'an).

Cheng Zhao (Yang Zheng) was born in 259BC, the son of King Zhuang Xiang of Qin by a concubine of a statesman Lu Buwei. His father died three years after ascending the throne, so that Cheng ascended the throne at the age of thirteen. During the early years of his reign the state was administered by his prime minister Lu Buwei, the man whom Cheng's mother once served as a concubine.

When old enough to be a ruler in his own right Cheng proved to be an exceptional person; from 230BC to 221BC he conquered most of China, 'all the land under heaven', renamed himself first emperor Qin Shihuang and installed a harsh bureaucracy to administer his great agrarian empire. From his capital Xi'an, Qin Shihuang saw the Great Wall completed and in his quest for immortality had a huge tomb built, guarded by an army of life-size terracotta warriors and horses, well over 8000 strong, buried rank after rank, adjacent to his tomb and just outside Xi'an.

The Qin dynasty did not last long and was subsequently followed by the Western Han who ruled China from Xi'an for two centuries. They built a city wall twenty-six kilometres in circumference and on the orders of the then emperor, the imperial envoy Zhang Qian was despatched to the western region to open up the Silk Road to Persia and Rome. Under the Western Han, Xi'an soon ranked with Rome as one of the most important world cities; Xi'an was in fact a metropolis at the time of Christ. Later under the Sui and Tang dynasties, 580ad to 906ad the city reached its second golden age, equalling Constantinople in importance and size.

Although no longer China's capital, Xi'an remains the capital of China's north-west province of Sha'anxi. In the vicinity are fossilised bones, 850,000 years old, indicating that once Homo erectus (Lanthan man) roamed the valley, and much, much later archaeological evidence attests to settled life 7000 years ago during the new stone age. To this day the Chinese government has refused permission to excavate Qin Shihuang's massive tomb.

Smaller than Peking, Shanghai and Nanjing, the city remains an important gateway to China's northwest and remains home to some of China's most beautiful treasures. Today many regard Xi'an as the cultural and historical capital of China.

References: China Pictorial Publications (ed.), *The Silk Road on Land and Sea (Beijing, China Pictorial Publications, 1989)*.

Patricia Buckley Ebery, *Cambridge Illustrated History*, (London, Cambridge University Press, 1990).

Edmund Capon, *Qin Shihuang: The Terracotta Warriors and Horses (Publication arranged by the Art Gallery of NSW, 1983)*.

It was a remarkable achievement and although deep suspicions

remained it was the first time that the Chinese had formed a united front against the Japanese and it was due to one man, the thirty four year old son of a Manchurian warlord.

Chiang Kai-shek was furious; he felt that final victory against the communist was in his grasp (which may well have been true) and he never forgave Zhang Xuelang for forcing him to accept them as allies.

The Young Marshall was flown to the capital Nanjing (Nanking) to face a court marshal. He was found guilty and sentenced to ten years' imprisonment. This was rescinded by Chiang Kai-shek who arranged for him to be placed under indefinite house arrest.

His first place of detention was a three storey mountain hostel in a picturesque area of Ningbo. There were peach blossoms in the garden and nearby was a laughing Buddha Temple said to be 1500 years old. Six months later a fire destroyed the hostel and Zhang moved into quarters within the temple. Down the hill lay the village where Chiang Kai-shek had been born fifty years before. Chiang had certainly chosen a peaceful place for his most illustrious prisoner, a person to whom he owed much but could not forgive for what had happened at Xi'an.

During the second civil war in China (after 1945) Zhang was moved from place to place, always under house arrest, before being flown to Taiwan in 1949 with Chiang Kai-shek. While under house arrest he spent his time studying Ming Dynasty poetry. In 1990 he was released. He converted to Christianity, married his long-time lover and companion and moved to Hawaii where he died in 2001 at the age of one hundred.

In the end Zhang Xuelang the Young Marshal outlived them all: Chiang Kai-shek, Mao, Chou En-lai, Madam Chiang Kai-shek, the Emperor Pi Yu and the Japanese generals who stole his country.

After regaining his freedom in 1990 there were numerous pleas for him to visit mainland China, but Zhang claiming his political neutrality, always declined to do so; perhaps he did not quite trust them! He never saw his beloved Manchuria again.

Reference: Jonathan Fenby, *Generalissimo and the China He Lost*, (East Roseville, Simon & Schuster, 2002).

Silk

Silk is the thread produced by the caterpillar of the silkworm moth, which feeds on leaves of the mulberry tree and spins a silken cocoon containing 900 metres of thread. To produce one kilogram of silk requires 50,000 cocoons.

There seems to be no doubt that the Chinese were the first to produce silk and were doing so over 5000 years ago. How they acquired this skill is not known, but legends about silk abound in China. One of the most popular stories has it that way back when the earth was young, the goddess of the silkworm descended from heaven and presented the Yellow Emperor (the progenitor of the Chinese) with a bundle of white silk to commemorate his victory over King Chiyou. The emperor passed this gift onto his wife the empress Lei Zu who learnt how to cultivate mulberry trees, breed silkworms and weave the shimmering cloth. It was Lei Zu who passed this knowledge down to her ladies in waiting.

Chinese silk was taken to other lands in very early times; to Westerners it was a mysterious and valuable fabric demanding a huge price and became a must for the wealthy in Rome. According to the Roman scholar Pliny the Elder, the Romans spent huge amounts of money on Chinese silk each year.

To carry this precious fabric to the west caravans crossed some of the most inhospitable lands in Asia. Initially caravan routes to Burma, India and the Aral Sea were developed well before the great Silk Road was surveyed by Zhang Qian during the second century AD. This great Silk

Road, once established, stretched 6400 kilometres from China to the Mediterranean. Westward went silk, cotton, jade and porcelain; and eastward went wool and precious metals.

With the fall of Rome and later the Byzantine Empire, trade declined, although the Silk Road was still in use during the Middle Ages when Marco Polo travelled to China to visit the great Khan. Its importance declined further with the opening up of sea trade between Europe and China in the late fifteenth century. Nevertheless, the road remains as a communicating route to central Asia and recently a railway, and pipeline 3750 kilometres long has been laid along the bed of the old Silk Road from China to Kazakhstan.

Reference: China Pictorial Publications (ed.), *The Silk Road on Land and Sea (Beijing, China Pictorial Publications, 1989).*

China's Great Wall extended westward from the Yellow Sea, passing north of Peking for 2500 km inland. Building began in the second century BC, *with extensive rebuilding during the fifteenth and sixteenth centuries.*

In 1924, Zhang pushed south of the wall and occupied Peking. The photo is of the Tien An Min Gate, one of the entrances to the Imperial City.

Zhang Xuelang, the 'Young Marshall'. He forced Chiang Kai-shek to deal with Mao and present a united front against the Japanese. (Generalissimo and the China He Lost, Jonathan Fenby, Simon & Schuster)

Mao. In the end he conquered China, an area of 3.7 million square miles and established the 'People's Republic of China' on October 1949.

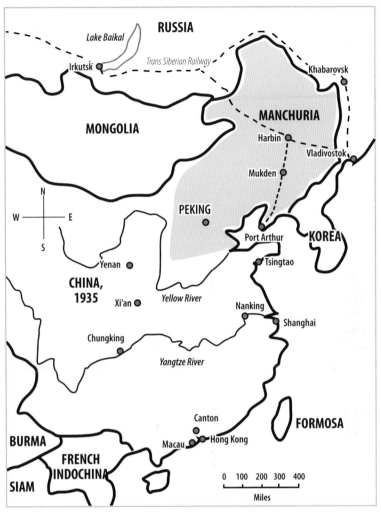

The author's map showing the extent of land controlled by the 'Old Marshall', Zhang Zhoulin in 1924, marked in yellow

CHAPTER 28

Copper

Copper

Jack Ellis and I have just returned from a duck-shooting weekend at Mai Po Swamps. We have been shooting partners for a number of years and we probably know the ins and outs of that area better than most.

It is an interesting bit of territory, bordering the Castle Peak Road to the north, reaching Deep Bay, covering the Sim Chun River flats and the entire length of land between the river and the road.

There are lots of rice fields, especially around Ping Shan and Yuen Long, where snipe migrate in the season. There are ducks around Mai Po swamps and along the length of the river as well as on the opposite side of the Deep Bay. Kam Tin Valley is also good for snipe. What is now the Fanling golf course was once a good place for snipe and partridge, but with the club activities this has petered off to some extent.

We arrived too late on Saturday afternoon for it to be any good for snipe, but we installed ourselves as usual in Ah Poh's chilly tool shed. One of his sons was on duty; he had built a useful fire (it was a cold night) and had the latest information on the state of the duck population.

Ah Poh runs a series of prawn ponds and I always find these quite interesting. The prawns march along the seabed in shallow water and when the tide is right, or the moon is in the right quarter, they wheel right or left as their fancy takes them and march in through the sluice gates where they are scooped up for market.

We had made arrangements to borrow one of Ah Poh's sampans for the night's shooting exercise, which turned out to be not particularly successful. Unfortunately we have only the one retriever, Bruno, who belongs to Jack; as mine has been naughty and is AWL this weekend. Jack's dog is quite good but has one rather serious fault: he is unable to distinguish between wild and domestic ducks and the result is not always a happy one. Poor old Bruno looks so very stupid when he comes waddling along the river grass with a large domestic fowl in his mouth!

My own dog, Copper, is in disgrace and for this reason we are calling at Mai Po Police Station tomorrow to pick him up. Some two weeks ago I was shooting over near Mai Po and called on Sergeant Cotton, who told me that Sally, his bitch, was on heat and was locked up in one of the police cells for the time being. I had Copper with me and, needless to say, he was greatly interested and had to be more or less forcibly taken home with us on Sunday night.

Well, on Monday, after that visit two weeks ago, Copper went missing. I advertised of course without result and enquiries were to no avail, so I began to get worried until Sergeant Cotton phoned me from Mai Po. 'I saw your advertisement,' he said, 'about Copper. He is here of course; has been here for a week, a damned nuisance. You'd better come out during the weekend and pick him up.'

So we began to piece together his (i.e. Copper's) movements from the time he left home, half-way up the Peak, on Hong Kong Island. He probably ran down from the Peak to the Star Ferry terminal and took the ferry across the harbour to the Canton Railway Station where he boarded a train to Fanling. We checked on this with the station attendant who knows the dog and saw him board the train. He got off the train at Lo Wu and legged it for the rest of the distance, some three or four miles, to finally reach his amorous Sally – with the usual love duet.

Our shoot at Mai Po was quite successful; we brought back a respectable bag. Three teal, two ducks, four couples of snipe and a couple of scale back pigeons who got themselves mixed up with the party.

So we were quite happy when we turned the car towards the police station to pick up the lovelorn Copper who was howling his head off in a cell.

Sergeant Cotton, an understanding gentleman, lost no time getting the rum bottle out and it was wonderful after the miserable night we had spent in the sampan. He called in his senior Indian constable and ordered the largest and fattest capon they had in the compound for curry, which in due time arrived on the table with Chu patties, freshly made. The curry was enough to make tears roll down my cheeks and by the time we left, we were feeling nicely reconditioned. Even Copper was quiet on the homeward trip after his strenuous week with Sally.

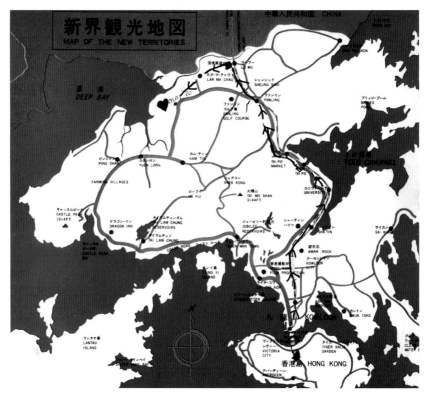

Copper's journey to Sally

Sverre Berg, 1930s

PART EIGHT

JAPAN'S WAR, 1941

CHAPTER 29

The Rising Sun

Fukoku Kyohei (National Wealth and Military Strength)

Why Japan attacked the colonial powers in 1941 is not well known. The signs, however, were there for all to see. Unfortunately we Europeans were too absorbed with the events unfolding in Europe.

It all began in 1852.

Commodore Matthew C. Perry, commander of the United States naval forces in the China seas was a staunch expansionist. In 1852 he wrote to President Fillmore warning him that the British, who had already taken control of Hong Kong and Singapore, would soon control all trade in the area. Perry recommended that the USA take 'active measures to secure a number of ports of refuge in Japan'.

President Fillmore agreed with Perry. In 1853 he ordered the commodore to open negotiations with Japan and provided Perry with a personal and friendly letter to the emperor.

In 1853 Perry, in charge of a squadron of four warships, anchored in Edo Bay (Tokyo); and after some haggling, the letter requesting moderate trading rights was handed over. It was agreed that Perry should return in 1854 to receive the reply.

During the sixteenth century and long before Perry entered Edo Bay, venturesome Portuguese, Dutch and English merchant seamen had opened up trade with Japan. They were soon followed by Catholic missionaries who introduced Christianity, which proved popular.

All this changed following the death of Hideyoshi (1598), the virtual ruler of Japan. Power now fell into the hands of the Tokugawa family. Under the Tokugawa shogunate a strict isolationist policy was introduced, which lasted for 270 years. Now overseas trade could only be conducted through one port, Nagasaki, and only by the Dutch. Foreigners could not venture outside Nagasaki. Japanese could not travel overseas. Only coastal vessels could be built, and Christianity was suppressed.

This was the situation in Japan when Perry defied Japanese law, bypassed Nagasaki and dropped anchor in Edo Bay. Perry's mission to open trade with Japan was not to be an easy one. Fillmore's letter was addressed to the emperor, the then spiritual leader of Japan and not to the ruling Tokugawa shogun, the true temporal rulers of the country. To further complicate matters, the current emperor was terminally ill and died shortly after the letter was delivered. His successor, the Emperor Komei was faced with the task of replying to the letter, knowing full well the rules of trade laid down by the Tokugawa. In 1854 Perry as agreed returned, this time with eight ships to receive a rather non-committal reply to Fillmore's letter. Nevertheless, after some haggling an agreement of sorts was reached. Not surprisingly, other colonial powers were quick to follow the Americans. Trading rights were agreed upon and treaties signed with Britain (1854), Russia (1855) and Holland (1856).

The Tokugawa shogun did not take kindly to this interference and the Japanese did not comply with the spirit of the agreements. In 1865 an allied squadron made up of British, French, Dutch and American ships anchored off Kyoto and by this show of power forced the ratification of the treaties.

It was at this time that the Tokugawa shogunate began to lose power. There was much poverty in Japan and a great deal of unrest. As a result the Satsuma, Choshu and other clans were able to unite and overthrow the Tokugawa and install the emperor as both the spiritual and temporal leader of Japan. This was the Meiji Restoration. Although in theory the emperor now had a dual role, real power still lay with an oligarchy made up of old families, Daimyos and Samurai.

The newly installed emperor Prince Mutsuhito was the surviving son of Emperor Komei. He ascended the throne in February 1867 at the age of fourteen and immediately became the symbolic leader of the

Meiji Restoration (enlightened rule). Mutsuhito reigned for forty-five years, had fifteen children by five different court ladies but none by his wife the empress. His 45-year reign is known as the Meiji period, during which far reaching changes occurred in Japan.

Isolationist policies were abandoned, the country was opened up to foreign trade, foreign ideas embraced and industries developed. The emperor moved from his traditional seat at Kyoto to Edo now renamed Tokyo and the ancient and traditional Shinto religion (the way of the gods) declared the state religion.

The Way of the Gods

During the first millennium BC several clans migrated from north eastern Asia and settled in Japan. By doing so they displaced the indigenous Ainu people, who moved to the more remote parts of the islands.

Initially mutually antagonistic to each other, each clan developed a rich and varied store of myths and legends based mainly on natural phenomena and objects, described as 'an amorphous mix of nature worship, fertility cults, divination techniques, hero worship and shamanism'. In time the clans became more united and their primitive beliefs coalesced into a single religion Shinto.

Like most religions Shintoism tries to explain creation and lays down a set of guidelines for the faithful.

To explain creation, Shintoism teaches that in the beginning a divine couple created the Japanese islands, which are therefore sacred. These islands also gave birth to the kami or deities. The most important of these deities was the Sun Goddess Amaterasu, the creator of the first emperor, Jimmu. Amaterasu is still worshipped in the Imperial Temple of Ise. This is of course no more incredible than making the earth in six days, walking on water or making a woman from a man's rib. The present emperor Akahito (2007AD) is the 125th descendent of Jimmu.

Shinto teaches that all humanity is a child of a Kami and therefore sacred and fundamentally good but unfortunately plagued by evil spirits. The purpose of most Shinto rituals is therefore to help keep these evil spirits at bay. Shinto beliefs include a reverence for ancestors, sincerity, a respect for family, loyalty to one's rulers, a love of nature, physical cleanliness and peace. Buddhism and Confucian teachings were introduced into Japan from China during the seventh century AD and easily coexisted with Shintoism.

Declared the state religion during the Meiji Restoration, Shintoism was disestablished after

Japan was defeated in World War II. Nevertheless, Shinto beliefs remain deeply imbedded in many Japanese. Over 80,000 public shrines remain and many Japanese families have their own little shrines in their homes.

Reference: Peter Bishop and Michael Darton, *The Encyclopaedia of World Faiths* (London and Sydney, McDonald Orbis, 1987).

The Russian Baltic fleet sailed halfway around the world to be destroyed by the Japanese fleet at Tsushina in 1905.
It was the largest Naval battle of the pre-dreadnaught era.

Japan's modernisation was so successful that a state was created powerful enough to embark upon an expansionist policy, defeating China in 1894–1895 and Russia in 1904–1905 and thereby annexing Formosa (Taiwan) and Korea as well as gaining considerable influence in Manchuria.

Japan sided with Great Britain in World War I and as a result obtained Tsingtao (which was later given back to China) as well as the Caroline, Marshall and Mariana Islands from Germany at the Peace Conference in 1919.

In spite of these gains, the Japanese faced immense problems during the 1920s. Japan with 2900 people per square mile of usable farmland was the most crowded nation in the world, so that Japan's need for living space and raw material were acute. At that time, much of Asia's riches was in the grip of Western nations. Burma and Malaya with their deposits of rubber, tin, tungsten and bauxite belonged to Great Britain; Indochina's rubber plantations were held by France; the East Indies' vast oil reserves were controlled by the Dutch.

Japanese, knowing their country was the most advanced in all Asia with industries expanding and needing more and more raw materials, felt they had a right to these riches; indeed many felt they had a divine mission to redirect these riches back to Asia. As a result, Japanese politicians introduced the policy of a Greater East Asia Co-Prosperity Sphere.

The Japanese who held the deepest feelings about their nations problems and in particular their inability to control the sources of raw materials and the need for living space were young officers of the Imperial Army and Navy. They were furious at their leaders, who had signed agreements made at the Washington Conference in 1921–1922.

The Washington Conference involved Japan, China, America, Great Britain and other colonial powers. The purpose of the conference was to sort out future policies in the Far East and Pacific. The conference also addressed the question of relative naval strength. It was agreed that in future the ratio of capital ships (i.e. battleships) was to be USA five, Great Britain five and Japan three. Furthermore, capital ship size was to be limited to 35,000 tons. It was this naval agreement that particularly infuriated officers of the Imperial Japanese Navy. A measure of their fury was the assassination of two prime ministers and a finance minister during the early 1930s and, in spite of problems with the economy, a greater increase in the influence of the armed forces in government expenditure.

To the Japanese army the riches of Manchuria, Russia and China were the prime targets, but to the navy the riches of South East Asia, the Philippines and the Dutch East Indies were the prime targets. This meant that the army's objectives could only be achieved by defeating China and Russia, while the navy's objectives could only be achieved by defeating Great Britain, American, France and the Dutch. These were formidable tasks.

During 1931–1932 the Japanese Kwantung Army, which since 1905 had by treaty been guarding Japanese interest throughout southern Manchuria, annexed the whole country without any direction from Tokyo and then, with Tokyo's blessing, established the puppet state of Manchukuo under the deposed last Chinese emperor, Puyi.

Perhaps some excuses could be advanced for Japan's actions. Manchuria, nominally part of China, had been during the earliest part of the twentieth century under the personal rule of two warlords popularly referred to as the 'Old and Young Marshals' and as a result had become something of a wild card, almost independent of China. Nevertheless, the League of Nations condemned the annexation of Manchuria but did nothing about it. Japan noting the league's objection and weakness withdrew from the League of Nations, the first nation to do so.

Since the suppression of the Boxers in 1900 by an international force, foreign troops had by agreement with the then Manchu government been stationed in the vicinity of Peking. This force included 4000 Japanese troops. In July 1937 a number of clashes occurred between the Japanese components of this peace-keeping force and Chinese troops in the vicinity of the Marco Polo Bridge near Peking. These clashes led to the second brutal and protracted Sino–Japanese War. This resulted in Japanese victories in Shanghai and the horrific 'Rape of Nanking', where more Chinese were killed and butchered than the total number killed as a result of the two atomic bombs dropped on Japan in 1945, a fact largely forgotten by the West. In fact the brutality meted out by the Japanese army in Nanking equals the horrors of Belsen and the purges carried out in Russia under Stalin.

During this second Sino-Japanese War, Japan endeavoured to cut off supplies to China by blockading the whole of the Chinese coastline excluding the foreign port of Hong Kong. The obvious result was that enormous quantities of arms destined for the Chinese army and estimated to be 60,000 tons per month, poured through the colony into China in spite of Japanese objections.

In 1938 Japanese troops captured Canton, sixty miles from Hong

Kong. This put the colony virtually in the front line. Japan now requested the right to ship arms to her own troops in southern China through Hong Kong, as the Chinese had been doing for some years. To the credit of the British government and in the absence of any American support, the Japanese request was rejected. Sadly Britain's resolve to resist Japanese demands were limited by events that were now unfolding in Europe.

In September 1939 the long-expected war in Europe finally broke out. The sudden collapse of France in June 1940 left the British Empire alone facing Germany and her allies. In these circumstances a war with Japan was unthinkable and further concession inevitable.

A weakened Britain, which had faithfully observed all the treaty limitations on armaments, was now facing a major European conflict alone and again without any American support, had now to bow to Japanese demands and suspend all arms shipments across frontiers they controlled into China (i.e. Hong Kong and Burma).

These restrictions were not particularly onerous for at this point the Cantonese spirit of enterprise reasserted itself and partly nullified the effect of Britain's boycott on supplies to China. A considerable smuggling trade across the border from Hong Kong into China involving petrol, arms and spare parts evolved with the benevolent neglect of the Hong Kong authorities.

During 1938 the United States seemed at last to be awakening to the Japanese danger. There was an increasing support for the Chinese army and Chiang Kai-shek, a 20 percent increase in naval appropriations, an embargo placed on military supplies to Japan and in October 1939 the US Pacific fleet was moved forward from San Diego to Pearl Harbour on the Hawaiian island of Oahu.

Back in 1936 Japan had concluded an 'Anticomintern Pact' with Germany and Italy. Following Hitler's success in the West in 1940, this pact was strengthened and replaced by the 'Tripartite Pact'. Under this agreement Japan recognised the leadership of Germany and Italy in the establishment of a new order in Europe, while Germany and Italy reciprocated in regard to Japan's 'Greater East Asia policies'. The parties also agreed to come to one another's aid if one of them were attacked by an outside power, meaning the USA.

On 6 September 1941 at the old Imperial Palace, a meeting was held before Emperor Hirohito of Japan. Present were the nation's highest ranking civilian and military officers. For two hours these men rose in turn, bowed to the emperor and described the desperate economic situation confronting the nation and blamed the US, Great Britain and the Netherlands for withholding raw materials from Japan.

In spite of some misgivings by the emperor and other moderates, it was resolved that if the diplomats of Japan's foreign offices could not persuade those ranged against them to lift their embargoes on raw materials, Japan would go to war and by a massive surprise attack, force a negotiated peace, that would leave Japan with all the riches of South East Asia and Manchuria.

The die was cast: the Japanese military machine was in power and from that date, 6 September 1941, the Pacific war was inevitable as was the fate of Hong Kong.

Reference: Winston S. Churchill, *The Second World War* (London, Cassell, 1949–1954).

Samurai

According to Japanese mythology Japan's first emperor Jimmu was a descendant of the sun goddess Amaterasu and enthroned in 660BC.

Although revered throughout Japan, the emperor's duties for the first 1000 years were mainly symbolic and the country was ruled by various militaristic rulers or shoguns who were supported by various numbers of daimyos or dukes.

During the twelfth century, two very powerful shoguns fought protracted and bitter wars over land and both called on their daimyos for support. To comply with their lords' demands, the daimyos recruited groups of élite warriors from amongst their more influential citizens; these were the first samurai.

The samurai soon evolved into a warrior cast with certain privileges and a strict adherence to the ethics of Bashido, which emphasised Confucian principles, loyalty, self-discipline and respectable behaviour. Honour and loyalty were so ingrained in the samurai that an honourable suicide 'seppuku' (usually by committing hara-kiri, literally the cutting of the belly) is always better than defeat or a life of failure.

In 1867 the Tokugawa shogunate was overthrown and replaced by the emperor who now became the true temporal ruler of Japan. In 1871 the emperor abolished the old feudal system and privileges of the samurai. Predictably this led to a revolt, which was successfully put down by forces loyal to the emperor so that in theory the samurai class officially ceased to exist. But entrenched ideas persisted and the culture lingered on.

During the 1920s and 1930s men occupying the upper ranks of the Japanese army, navy and air force were united by the samurai traditions, which required that its senior officers and their subordinates must die if need be for the military honour of Japan and the emperor. By doing so, each officer believed that after death he could then face his personal court of ancestors with confidence.

This code of conduct, when the principal weapons were the sword or bow and Japan was an isolated island, had little effect on her neighbours. But as Japan emerged from her long seclusion and her warriors acquired lethal weapons of hitherto unimaginable power, she became a threat to the whole of Asia and the western Pacific, and led in time to the invasion of China and the Pacific war.

Even today the samurai tradition lingers on. Honour is paramount; death is better than defeat or failure. Failure in business or even in an exam sometimes leads to suicide. For these reasons Japan has the highest suicide rate in the world.

To track along the China coast during the 1930s
ships had to be well marked. DB

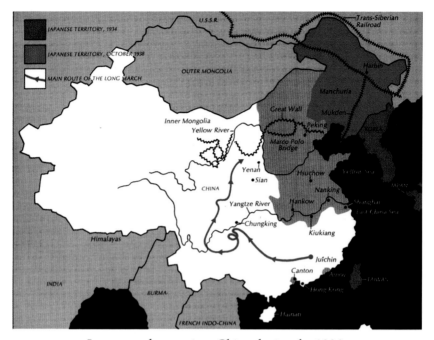

*Japanese advances into China during the 1930s
and the route of the long march*

CHAPTER 30

Twilight in Hong Kong

'A boat' or dragon class yacht, Hong Kong, 1941

On Saturday 6 December 1941 the usual Saturday race meeting was held at Happy Valley. Following the races the usual cocktail parties were on this occasion a little restricted simply because many were to attend the charity ball too be held at the Peninsula Hotel.

The ball was a great success, with 600 guests, the Governor and his Lady, beautifully gowned women and elegant men. Champagne flowed, there was much gaiety while across the harbour Hong Kong shone like a Christmas tree.

Sunday morning 7 December (Hong Kong time) was a glorious day and as on all Sundays in the far-flung colonies there was church parade. The Royal Scots piped their way to their kirk while men of the First Middlesex followed their regimental band to the Anglican Cathedral. Everything was as it had been in Hong Kong for nearly a hundred years. Sadly, it was to be their last church parade for a very long time.

Reference: Ellen Field, *Twilight in Hong Kong* (London, Frederick Muller, 1960).

O utside on that beautiful harbour, the most important yacht race sailed annually between the Scandinavians and British was to take place, no matter what the threat from across the boarder.

Four A-class boats (Dragon Class boats) crewed by Englishmen (three men per boat) were ranged against four A class boats crewed by Scandinavians. Of the twenty-four men involved in that race, sadly, five were to die before Christmas.

But this story is not a memorial to the dead; they will be certainly remembered and missed when we compete again and the starter's gun is once more the only disturbing bang that shatters the Sunday morning peace in Hong Kong. This is the story of that last race before Japan invaded Hong Kong.

The eight yachts manoeuvred for the start. The weather was perfect, a typical clear December morning when Hong Kong is at its best. The Monsoon was fairly strong from the north east. There had been talk amongst the 'experts' of reefing the main sails but none did and they crossed the starting line with full canvas.

They were all well bunched when Holger Dreyer (the Great Dane), skipper of *Redshank*, the leader of the Scandinavian team, began having trouble with his jib-halyard, which parted shortly after the start and the sail came sliding down its stay. By the time they got this fixed they were merely 'also rans'. Undaunted, the Great Dane decided this was an occasion that called for something more drastic than just following the others – so they downed helm and stood right across Hong Kong harbour, towards the Kowloon side, and as happens now and again success went to the brave for although they didn't clear Dock Point in their scrabble across the harbour, they found a more northerly breeze coming out of Kowloon Bay, which enabled them to lay the first mark, Channel Rocks, comfortably on port tack. They raced hell for leather for it whilst most of the fleet were still short tacking on the Hong Kong side; then some skippers noted what the Great Dane was doing over Kowloon side and started across – but too late. *Redshank* rounded the mark well in the lead – according to her skipper, 300 yards in front of the second boat *Guri,* whose crew, however, only conceded half this distance!

On the run back to the north point mark the lead was reduced a little, but not dangerously so. On the following beat, *Guri* gained a little, at least her helmsman said so, but *Redshank* remained well ahead and seemed to have the race well in her locker.

Then on the run back to the finishing line the Great Dane faced a potential disaster – a tug towing a number of barges right across his path – and with the breeze lightening he could not sail clear. *Guri* was catching up and at one time it seemed as if she would overtake him but that was not to be. Blue smoke issued up from *Redshank,* generated from three Nordic throats as they swore, cursed and threatened the tug boat skipper, who soon appreciated the gravity of the situation and the danger to his bodily wellbeing if he didn't do something quickly. He steered away sufficiently to allow *Redshank* through. Even so, *Guri,* who had gone further out, found a better breeze. She might have won had she carried a more experienced crew; they fumbled with the spinnaker, which did not set and one of their crew, standing on the foredeck, found part of the sail wrapped around his body like a toga. They could not get the sail free and ended up by splitting it in two halves – there it hung, still doing some good, but not what a spinnaker should do. After that there was no hope and *Redshank* romped across the line some sixty feet ahead to get the gun.

Two of the Scandinavians finished behind the British *Guri*; so with a first, third and fourth, it was enough; Scandinavia won.

Sadly, more mightier matters were stirring, and on their return to the club house (Royal Hong Kong Yacht Club) mobilisation orders were waiting, so the yachting caps were tucked away and replaced by head gear of a considerably drabber hue and the tiller gave place to a deadlier weapon.

The cup, we hope is still there, if not, well, we will always find something to take its place; if necessary we will polish up a brass cuspidor, place it on a plinth and race for it.

Reference: Sverre Berg, *Sam Shui Po – Christmas 1942.*

Holger Dreyer's problem

CHAPTER 31

DEFENDING HONG KONG

'In the first six to twelve months of a war with the United States and Britain, I will run wild and win victory after victory. After that I have no expectations of success'
Admiral Isoroku Yamamoto – Commander Combined Imperial Fleet

The position of Hong Kong should war with Japan break out, had been the subject of discussions by the British government. In January 1941 Churchill, then Britain's prime minister, had written to General Ismay, C in C Far East, who had been urging that substantial reinforcements be sent to the colony.

If Japan goes to war with us, there is not the slightest chance of holding Hong Kong or relieving it. It is most unwise to increase the loss we shall suffer there...

Churchill was right of course, but it was of no comfort to the soldiers, volunteers and civilians who fought and died defending the colony. Nevertheless, two Canadian battalions were sent to reinforce the army in Hong Kong.

To defend Hong Kong there were initially four regular army battalions, the 2nd Royal Scots, the 1st Middlesex, the 5/7 Rajputs and the 2/14 Punjabis. To this must be added the two Canadian battalions, the Winnipeg Grenadiers and the Royal Rifles of Canada. Both Canadian battalions had been previously on garrison duty in the West Indies and New Foundland, they were not seasoned troops and arrived in Hong

Kong less than a month before Japan attacked and without much of their equipment.

A reasonable standard of coastal defence was in place to defend against a naval attack (which was never to materialise). This included old pattern 9.2 inch guns and more up to date six-inch pieces.

Every battalion was equipped with three-inch mortars, but no ammunition until a shipment arrived in November 1941 and then only seventy rounds per battalion, enough for five minutes of intense bombardment. Battalions were also equipped with two-inch mortars, the vicious baby brother of the three-inch mortars, but without any ammunition. Close infantry support was supplied by a regiment of Royal Artillery equipped with old fashioned guns.

The naval contingent consisted of one old destroyer HMS Thracian with three four-inch guns and a top speed of twenty knots, one river gunboat HMS Cicala with two six-inch guns and six motor torpedo boats. The Air Force consisted of four Vickers torpedo bombers, without torpedoes, and three Supermarine Walrus Amphibians.

To this inadequate and poorly equipped force of regulars were added the Royal Hong Kong Volunteers. This partially volunteer force had been in existence for many years, with their own headquarters, stores and reasonable equipment. In 1940 British citizens not already serving were conscripted into the force, but men of over fifteen different nationalities voluntarily joined, including the one time Consul for Norway, Sverre Berg, who was made a gunner and attached to a six-inch coastal defence gun at Stanley Fort.

There are all sorts of stories told of those men that made up the RHKV. There were businessmen, bankers, engineers, rich men, poor men, teetotallers and alcoholics. Their ages ranged from nineteen to sixty-five. Some had their chauffeurs drive them to training, others took their houseboys on weekend bivouacs, but all were prepared to face 60,000 battle hardened and ruthless Japanese troops. Some sadly died horrible deaths.

On Beverages

The horse and mule live thirty years
And nothing knows of wines or beers.
The goat and sheep at twenty die
Without a taste of rum or rye.
The cow drinks water by the ton
At eighteen she is mostly done.
The dog at fifteen cashes in
Without the aid of ale or gin.
The cat in milk and water soaks
And in twelve short years it croaks.
The modest, sober, bone-dry hen
Lays eggs for men, then dies at ten.
All animals are strictly dry –
Sinless they live, and swiftly die.
But sinful, gin-full, rum-soaked men
Survive for three score years and ten
And some of us, the lucky few
Stay pickled till we're ninety-two!

Anon.

The Japanese attacked Hong Kong at dawn on Monday 8 December 1941 (i.e. 7 December, Honolulu time). This attack was launched simultaneously with the attack on Pearl Harbour.

The Japanese employed three divisions for the attack on Hong Kong, about 60,000 seasoned, well-equipped troops who had been toughened through years of fighting in Manchuria and China.

The Hong Kong forward defence line had been established in the New Territories and was euphemistically referred to as the 'Gin Drinkers Line', stretching for seventeen kilometres across the New Territories. To man this defence line were 2000 men comprising the Royal Scots, Punjabis and Rajputs. The Middlesex, Canadians and RHKV were retained on Hong Kong Island.

CHAPTER 32

My War with Japan

Sverre Berg, 1940

Operation Weserübung

During the 1930s German industry was heavily dependent on the import of iron ore from the northern Swedish mining district and much of this ore was shipped south to Germany through the northern Norwegian port of Narvik. In addition if war should eventuate with Britain, control of the long Norwegian coast would provide Germany with sea and air bases to challenge Britain for control of the North Sea.

These facts were recognised by both the British and German admiralties and both sides considered plans to occupy Norway.

There was however a complicating factor. In 1939 war broke out between Russia and Finland and both Britain and France considered sending men and material across northern Norway and Sweden to aid the Finns. This plan obviously required the agreement of both the Norwegian and Swedish governments. Both governments refused. Germany however was now well aware of Britain's interest in Norway.

Convinced of the threat posed by the allies to the iron ore supplies from Sweden, Hitler ordered plans to be drawn up for the invasion of Norway and Denmark. This plan was referred to as Operation Weserübung.

The German invasion began in early April 1940, but the sinking of the German heavy cruiser *Blücher* together with the resistance put up by the Oscarsborg fortress allowed the Norwegian royal family, the parliament and the national gold reserve to be evacuated from Oslo and moved to northern Norway. Norwegian forces, however, were no match to the German army and the British naval counter attack after some early successes failed.

As a result of failures to stem the German advance, the Norwegian royal family and parliament were evacuated from Tromso aboard the British cruiser HMS *Devonshire* and set up a government in exile in London. The Germans in their turn set up a Norwegian puppet government under Vidkum Quisling.

Norway was now in the eyes of the Western allies at war with Germany and later with Japan. Sverre Berg was no longer a neutral.

I am part of 'A Section' manning a six-inch gun at Port Stanley on the southern shore of Hong Kong Island. We are all Royal Hong Kong Volunteers; there are thirteen of us made up of men from six separate nationalities. Our ages range from nineteen to fifty-five. We are a happy crowd, inclined to look upon ourselves as bloody fine gunners, itching to get at the wily Nips.

Our battery is not involved in the fighting on the Kowloon side; our interest is focused on the Japanese destroyers off the coast. We can see three of them, one in each gap between the islands. They are part of the naval force blockading Hong Kong and remain well out of range. There have been a couple of alarms but nothing serious.

We have, however, been subject to plenty of air raids and as we have nothing better than Lewis guns to pop at them they can afford to be cheeky and fly very low over us. We watch them as they come in from the sea, generally half a dozen at a time. It is a nerve wracking business if you are at the receiving end of repeated low level bombing and strafing raids. In spite of the fact that there is virtually no opposition, they never seem to cause much damage. We can see their bombs leaving the planes and soon we become quite expert in gauging where they are likely to land. They never seem to do any damage to the guns. Of course many of their planes fly over the peak to Hong Kong proper and we can hear their bombs going off in the city.

To the west of us is Aberdeen, where the motor torpedo boats are stationed; they receive a lot of attention from the Japanese planes and there seems to be an almost permanent pall of smoke over the place.

Our six-inch gun is always ready with a shell up its spout, the rammer in the breach in place of the cartridge, all set, just replace the rammer with a cartridge, close the breach, lay the gun, press the trigger and we send 100 pounds of high explosive sailing through the air with our hopes that it may land fair and square on the target.

Our main problem is fatigue and tiredness. There is always something to do: shifting camouflage, digging trenches, cleaning out the shelter and adjusting the ventilation. We do the afternoon watch, then in relays of four we go to the kitchen for chow at 1800 hours, then back to the gun on stand-by duty till midnight. We are not allowed to sleep when on stand-by but can rest in the gun shelter in full kit. After midnight we are back on full duty again; our only rest is five hours in the morning after dawn.

This lack of sleep dulls our brains and a deadly lethargy creeps over us. We wait with dread for our turn at look-out because we know our eyes are playing tricks and this is not good. Last night I was on look-out from 3 am to dawn. A chilly, drizzly, miserable night. I was tired after eight sleepless nights; my legs were wobbly. One moment I imagined I saw the lights of a fleet of ships steaming in; the next moment nothing but the blackness of hell and an overpowering wish to lie down. I leaned against the gun shield; it was difficult to stand upright. I forced myself to walk up and down in front of the gun.

When the night draws to its inevitable end, we are ordered to our gun positions for an hour of 'miss fire' drill before marching off for five hours rest which includes food and a wash.

*   *   *

One can only speculate what this intelligent man thought as he paced to and fro in front of that gun on those lonely, miserable nights. There was little hope for Hong Kong and what of his wife? Alone in her house above the burning city? Stories of Japanese atrocities must be filtering through; was his own fate to be decided by a bayonet?

At 10 pm on the night of 18 December the Japanese landed on Hong Kong Island initiating the most terrible week in the colony's history.

The initial fury of Colonel Tanaka's 229th regiment fell on the fifth anti-aircraft battery manned by a section of the Royal Hong Kong Volunteers. Twenty-nine men were surrounded, forced to surrender and then bayoneted one by one as they emerged from the battery bunker, the hideous process went on till twenty-nine torn and bloody bodies lay on the ground; the lucky ones, stabbed in the throat, heart or liver died quickly; but others less fortunate were butchered and died more slowly. The bodies were then thrown into a ditch; quite remarkably two were not dead and survived the war.

The brutality continued for the next seven days; nurses were raped, doctors shot, patients bayoneted in their hospital beds and men that surrendered were killed one way or another.

Within seven days it was all over. On Christmas day 1941 the Hong Kong government surrendered. On the last day of fighting Gunner Sverre Berg of the Royal Hong Kong Volunteers was wounded while defending a six-inch gun at Fort Stanley. He recovered, spent the war as a POW at Sham Shie Po and in 1946 with Tui, his adoring wife (who was interned in Hong Kong), was repatriated to Sydney in a Royal Navy aircraft carrier.

When I saw them, they were sitting together, alone, drawn and thin with one small old battered suitcase and a carry bag in the huge hanger of that aircraft carrier. It was all they had left of their worldly possessions but inside them was a determination to start again and to succeed.

Reference: Frank Walsh, *A History of Hong Kong* (London, Harper Collins, 1994). Tim Carew, *The Fall of Hong Kong* (London, Pan Books, 1960).

An Encounter with Angels

'There are more things in heaven and earth Horatio then are dreamt of in your Philosophy'
– Shakespeare

On 22 August 1914, over 30,000 British regulars (including men of the Middlesex regiment) dug themselves in amongst the canals, pitheads and slag heaps of the drab little Belgium mining town of Mons and prepared to face the oncoming German first army. On Sunday 23 August the armies clashed, and at the height of that terrible battle amongst the smoke, drizzle and flying debris some of those hardened old British regulars saw angels above the battle field casting a protective curtain between them and the advancing enemy, allowing them to withdraw in good order.

Because of these sightings, an aura of mystique surrounds Mons and that opening engagement of World War I. The first battle fought in northern Europe by the British army since Waterloo (also in Belgium).

There is another story, little less known perhaps but very real to troopers of the Australian Light Horse. I am in debt to that wonderful book by Ion Idriess, *The Desert Column*. Idriess served as a trooper in the Australian Light Horse during the Desert Campaign.

On 23 December 1916 the Australian Light Horse occupied El Arish in northern Sinai and then immediately rode a further thirty miles to attack and defeat the Turks at Maghbada. After a bitter fight the Light Horse then embarked upon a further night ride back to base. I quote Idriess in full:

A very peculiar story is being discussed throughout the Desert Column. It appears that the troops when riding back the 30 miles from Maghbada were enveloped in blinding clouds of dust. Nearly the whole column was riding in snatches of sleep; no-one had slept for four nights and they had ridden 90 miles.

Hundreds of men saw the queerest of visions — weird looking soldiers were riding beside them, many were mounted on strange animals. Hoards walked right amongst the horses making not the slightest sound. The column rode through towns with lights gleaming from shuttered windows of quaint buildings. The country was all waving green fields and trees and flower gardens. Numbers of the men are speaking of what they saw in a most interesting, queer way. There were tall stone temples with marble pillars and swinging oil lamps – our fellows could smell the incense – and white mosques with stately mignonettes.

It is strange to hear the chaps discussing what they saw as they sit smoking under the palms. I don't think they would talk so openly had it not been for a general riding with his staff. Suddenly he and a companion officer galloped off into the darkness. It has just come out that both officers suddenly saw a fox and galloped after it. The men now don't mind telling what they saw, for when two of our 'heads' saw strange things, well.

Writers and theorists in their comfortable lounges have debunked the soldier's stories, putting the visions down to stress, terror and exhaustion. So that the angels of Mons became enshrined as one of the myths of World War I, but was it a myth? Who are we that were not there, not stressed, not terrified or exhausted to say that these men did not actually see angels that helped them to escape that carnage? Is it simply because we do not believe in miracles?

The appearance of the angels at Mons and the strange desert phantoms may or may not be real, but what is real happened to men also of the Middlesex regiment on the streets and sidewalks of Wanchai (downtown Hong Kong) on Christmas day 1941. On this occasion the angels were not in the sky, they did not have wings and they were not clothed in white. Instead, they wore gaily coloured cheongsams, slit up to the thigh; they were the mistresses, bar girls and dahnhomers of the non-commissioned officers and privates of the regular British army whose lot it had been to face inevitable defeat. As these soldiers lay wounded and dying on the streets and doorways of Wanchai, their angels came through the smoke and wreckage with bandages, looted cigarettes, food, water and even beer for the men that had been once part of their lives. They showed them warmth and even love in that short interval before the wounded were either bayoneted to death or herded into a POW camp.

Later many of these angels, perhaps loose and amoral women, risked brutal beatings by the Japanese for taking parcels to their men imprisoned behind wire. These men, lowly privates and NCOs of the old regular British army, had no-one else to care and comfort them. These women were the very real angels of Hong Kong.

References: Ion Idriess, Greatest Stories (North Ryde, NSW, Angus & Robertson, 1986).
Derek Berg, *My Paper Trail* (Nambour, Derek Berg, 2005).

Hong Kong under attack, 1941, painted by Japanese artist Hoshun Yamaguchi. The tower to the right is part of the railway terminus. To the left across the harbour is the Hong Kong and Shanghai Bank building, partly covered by smoke. (Time Life)

EPILOGUE

Áfter the war Sverre Berg with partners built up a small but successful shipping business in Australia. They bought and managed a number of small steamers, which carried cargoes to northern Queensland ports, Papua New Guinea and other Pacific Islands.

Sverre became an early and enthusiastic member of the Cruising Yacht Club of Australia. Bought a forty-foot ketch made of Huon Pine named *Horizon*. In her he competed in two Hobart Yacht Races, the Inaugural Sydney to Noumea classic and various shorter ocean events.

Sverre Berg died in the arms of his wife Tui at their home in Elanora Heights, Sydney on 11 March 1979. His ashes were consigned to the sea he loved at a point midway between Barrenjoey Lighthouse and Cape Three Points, sixteen nautical miles north of Sydney.

Sverre driving Horizon under full sail to Hobart

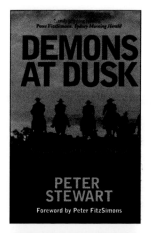

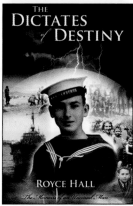

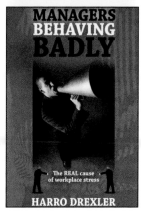

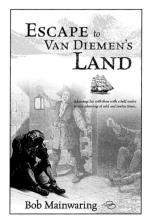

OTHER BEST SELLING SID HARTA TITLES CAN BE FOUND AT

http://sidharta.com.au   http://Anzac.sidharta.com

***

HAVE YOU WRITTEN A STORY?
http://publisher-guidelines.com

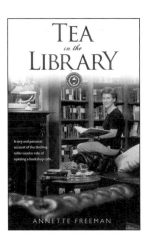
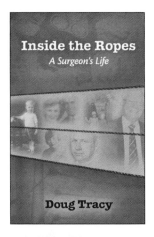

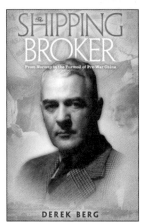

Best-selling titles by Kerry B. Collison

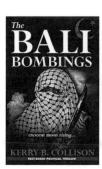   

Readers are invited to visit our publishing websites at:
http://sidharta.com.au
http://publisher-guidelines.com/

Kerry B. Collison's home pages:
http://www.authorsden.com/visit/author.asp?AuthorID=2239
http://www.expat.or.id/sponsors/collison.html
http://clubs.yahoo.com/clubs/asianintelligencesresources
email: author@sidharta.com.au

Purchase Sid Harta titles online at:
http://sidharta.com.au

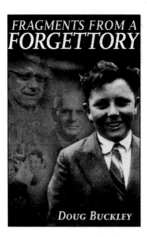
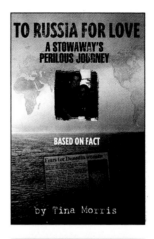

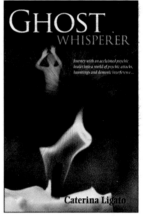